Shivendra Sharma

# BEING YOGI

## An Accidental Serendipity



BlueRose ONE
Stories Matter

**BLUEROSE PUBLISHERS**
India | U.K.



For permissions requests or inquiries regarding this publication, please contact:

BLUEROSE PUBLISHERS
www.BlueRoseONE.com
info@bluerosepublishers.com
+91 8882 898 898
+4407342408967

ISBN: 978-93-93384-14-0

Printed in INDIA

Cover design: Varsha Nagpal, Aman Sharma
Typesetting: Namrata Saini

First Edition: June 2023

*Dedicated to*

Mahavatar Babaji, whose inspiration led to this creation

# Acknowledgement

It took precisely 10 years to write this book. This is not just a book but an amalgamation of real experiences, spiritual encounters, memories and realization.

Having said this, there are a lot of people who inspired this journey to finally culminate in this book. This book goes through many phases of life and each phase had its lessons to be learnt.

So Mahavatar Babaji is the prime inspiration whose blessings led to these writings as a book.

Nothing in life moves without the blessings of parents. They have been the biggest support in my life and always believed in my stupidity in all forms.

My better half, Supriya, has been a constant motivator for me to keep writing and at times gave me honest feedback on some of the portions of the book.

I would like to acknowledge my close friends in Delhi and in Hyderabad whose blessings and excitement about the book motivated me to continue writing. If I start naming them, I might need to write another book, but their support has been immense.

My office colleagues have been very excited from the day one they got to know about the book. I am counting on them to make this a best seller.

Blue Rose publisher has been very supportive as their guidance and support have been critical factors to get to this point where you can read this. They are the final and the most important piece in this puzzle which helped me to put together this.

I can be reached out on my mail id for any feedback-

**shiv.isbm@gmail.com**

# Introduction

It took me 10 years to get to this stage where I am finally writing this piece. Many manuscripts were torn, and pages were thrown away. I just wanted to write something based on what inspired me. Ideas were plenty but they had no structure, or direction. This went on for almost 8 years and so did the life.

Experiences, memories and life kept happening. The book kept taking shape with each experience until one day everything started to fit perfectly in the overall puzzle. It seemed as if the book was waiting for all episodes to be completed before the climax.

And here we are, with the final product, which is a journey of guts, grit, determination, awakening and freedom from bondage.

A lot changed in these 10 years. You know what, when you complete the book, it is no more a book. You become the book yourself. The book embraces you as you see your life wrapped inside those pages. Just flip a few of them, and boom, you are traversing through the memory lanes.

Someone asked me if it is difficult to write a book. I replied, book writing is not difficult if you can face your demons in such a way that the whole world reads about it. I shall not divulge many details and will leave it for the readers to guess.

It has been a journey which does not end here. This gives me immense happiness and inspiration to present my first novel in front of the world.

"Being yogi" awaits you......

# About the Author

Shiven (That's how he is known among his friends) dons many hats in his life. He is a storyteller, a poet, a passionate singer, an avid reader and now an author.

Shiven lives in Hyderabad but his roots are from Bareilly, Uttar Pradesh. He has a successful career in corporate and worked with many global organizations in past where he worked in strategy consulting & business transformation.

# Contents

# CHAPTER 1

## The Old Man

**15th May 2018**

It was a fine evening. Sam was sitting in a nice pub with friends. Sam has always been the most vocal in every group and this group was no different. They have been discussing the economic policy of the Indian government. It can be easily guessed; they were all 3-4 pegs down. Everyone was the expert in this discussion. Rohit, Sam's old colleague said, "with this rate, we shall never be able to match with the might of China. We have to grow faster than them and at least 10% every year."

The first time since they started discussing, Sam seemed to agree with someone. However, this is unlike him. He always wants others to agree with him or follow him. He does not like to be told a fact or a reality. He constructs his own facts and reality and wants others to believe him. So, he was confused as he had to come back with a strong argument and prove Rohit wrong.

He was clueless so he ordered a strong peg of scotch whiskey, his favourite brand, Johnny Walker Double black. While the waiter took a few minutes to bring it, Sam was restless all this while and when he brought the whiskey, he almost pounced on him and shouted, "What took you so long to get a fucking peg of whiskey".

Bloody useless, lower class. All his colleagues looked at him with eyes wide open and wondered about this sudden burst of anger.

"Where did this come from, Sam", Preeti asked, another of Sam's colleagues.

"Is something bothering you? You have been quiet for some time now. This is unlike the Sam we know."

And then Sam was back to his senses. All he was looking for was retaliation or a reply to Rohit's argument.

He said with a grin on his face, "because of these people", he pointed towards one of the waiters, we shall never be able to match with China. Because if it takes this long to bring a peg of whiskey, imagine how they will fare in a highly competitive world. So, forget GDP Rohit, we need smarter, faster and intelligent people which I definitely don't see around me."

Rohit had known Sam for over 10 years now and he knew where this was coming from. But whiskey had done its charm and the battlefield was open now. He said, “You need to change your company Sam if you don’t see intelligent people around you”.

He paused for a while, took a long sip from his glass and put it back on the table. He laughed hard rather burst into laughter, put his left hand on Sam’s shoulder and winked at him and said, “Chill dude. We are meeting after so long. Fuck economic policy. How is your new job going on?”

The plot had been changed smartly by Rohit. He winked back at the group and went towards the restrooms without waiting for an answer from Sam. It was 12:30 AM and the bar was almost empty now. Monday night is not a fun night for everyone and definitely not for Preeti who recently gave birth to twins.

She suddenly announced the arrival of her cab, “Guys, I have booked my cab and it will arrive in 2 minutes. It was awesome meeting you all after so long. And Sam, you are an ass, but I still like meeting you. So, everyone, let’s keep meeting and keep this old group alive.” Sam nodded in agreement.

Sam, in his signature style, signalled the waiter to bring the bill. And this time he was looking at his watch and counting the minutes to be back to his natural self. Preeti noticed it and said, come on Sam, chill yaar. You always look for an opportunity or what. Leave the poor guy alone. Let them do their job for god’s sake. Sam smiled sheepishly and to his utter surprise, the waiter was waiting next to him with a card machine and bill.

He reached for his wallet to pay and then Preeti intervened. "Sam, we all are earning now" and winked at Rohit who was back from the restroom. They all burst into laughter.

They paid individually with their own cards. Preeti got up and hugged Sam & Rohit. While hugging Sam, she whispered in his right ear, it's ok to lose an argument sometimes and left immediately. While Sam was trying to understand, Rohit too announced the arrival of his cab. He hugged Sam and left right after.

Sam was alone now and heavily drunk. He had to drive back to his home. Typical Sam did not want to hire a cab or a driver.

Sam was lucky that night. He did not come across any drunk driving check on the way to his apartment. However, he had a strange encounter at a traffic signal. Midway to his home, he stopped at a traffic signal. It showed 220 seconds for the green light. "What a waste of time. And that asshole Rohit says we can compete with China. Every fucking place we have to wait, stand in a queue. Who the hell waits for 220 seconds on a fucking traffic signal at 1 AM?"

Knock, knock, someone knocked at the car window, to his side. He looked outside. It was not too bright, and he was not sober too, but he could see a pale, thin, old man with bright red eyes looking straight into his eyes. His gaze was piercing. For a moment, Sam was lost but he collected himself and shouted at that old man without opening the window. “Get lost, you beggar. In this country, beggars are everywhere, and traffic signals are like breeding grounds for them. This government is useless. Bloody scoundrels.”

That old man kept looking at Sam without saying anything and that made Sam furious even more. His gaze, Sam just could not avoid.

Honnkkkkkkk...A truck was honking from behind. The traffic signal had turned green. Sam looked outside again but the old man was gone. Like disappeared into thin air. Who cares about a beggar at a traffic signal in India at 1 AM. Sam reached home and crashed into his bed. He was too drunk to be awake further.

# CHAPTER 2

## *The Beginning*

**13th November 2008**

But was Sam always like that? Was he always so self-centred, ready to pounce on others and foul mouthed? The answer is NO. He was a different person until his experiences in life moulded him into an ass which Preeti called him.

If we traverse the path of memories, sometimes in 2008, some 10 years back, that is where it all began.

Samrat Bhagat, had completed one year in his first job. Fresh out of college. And to no one's surprise, he did not like a second of it. He hated that job and his boss. Though, his boss did not like either. For him, every day was a struggle to get ready, take the metro and reach the office. His only solace was his colleagues, who made him forget his struggles and hatred.

But if Samrat did not like his job, then what did he desire to do? He was a daydreamer. He always dreamt of having his own venture, being his own boss and living a life that he described as "The Uber Life", the life of a businessman, always on the go with lots of excitement and challenges. His dreams never had a starting point, an idea or a direction. It was just wishful thinking until one fine day he met someone, in the humid, dark but busy corridor of the same office he hated from his core.

Samrat was in the Human resources department and looked after the joining formalities & orientation of new employees who joined this firm. This guy he met that day in the corridor had joined a week back. Samrat could recognize him well as he belonged to the same city as Sam did. So, it was an instant connection.

"Hey Akshay", Samrat waved his hand to that guy. Akshay looked at Sam and he waved back. "How are you, buddy? Enjoying the new office?", "So far, so good. Can't complain yet'" Akshay said and they both burst into laughter.

"So, are you going to Kanpur on Diwali?" Sam asked Akshay. "No Yaar, a lot of work. Boss has given a lot of documents to read and prepare the brand strategy", Akshay replied.

"Who, that baldy? Dude, that guy is a real pain in the ass. God bless you", Sam said with a cheeky smile. Akshay could not help but smile.

"Any plans this evening after office?" Sam asked. "Nothing yet, you tell me," Akshay said.

“Let’s go to DROP, this lounge, opposite our office. Nice place it is, and you can meet pretty girls too” Samrat said, winking at Akshay.

“Sounds like a plan! let’s go. I shall try to finish work by 7 PM and ping you then. Will that work?” Akshay asked.

“Of course, buddy, let’s go to DROP and drop all our worries and frustration,” Sam said and they both burst into laughter again.

“Hello there”. Samrat got a ping on the office messenger. It was 7 PM sharp. The office was almost empty on Friday evening. He ignored it as a lot of employees used to ping him all day.

“Ready to DROP” was another ping and this time he had a smile on his face. He opened the chat and replied, “Sure, just dropping some stupid emails and then let’s drop together at DROP, sic. I shall see you at the lift lobby in 5 minutes”.

Samrat spent another 5 minutes at his desk, packed his bag and went towards the Washrooms.

“Wow, you too dropped here” Akshay was right next to him. “Hello stalker, there seems to be some weekend vibe intervention. We have been meeting just too often in one day” Samrat said, and both had a hearty laugh. Ok, I shall see you in the lift lobby in 2 minutes” Samrat said and left.

It was a windy and chilly winter evening in Delhi. December is when winter comes knocking in North India. Both crossed the road and landed straight into DROP. It was a beautiful lounge with live music, full of young corporate crowd from nearby offices. It was Samrat's usual hangout place. Whenever life got too boring or exciting, he would come here, sit, have a beer, look around and just sit and do nothing. Basically, he would contemplate his life decisions here. But today was a different day. He was not alone today.

"Beer or Whiskey" Sam asked Akshay. "Anything bro" Akshay replied.

"They don't serve anything here", Sam said and put his arm around Akshay's shoulder and took him to the bar counter.

"Do you see those beautiful bottles in Front of you Akshay? What do you see in them? Alcohol?``,"yes `` Akshay said.

"I see escape, my friend. An escape from reality, the world and all my problems" and he laughed so hard, he almost lost his balance.

"Ok, I will order Whiskey," Akshay said.

"That's my man, I will also order whisky," Samrat said and ordered two large pegs of Black Dog Scotch whiskey and sat near the bar counter only. This was Samrat's favourite corner as he could see the whole place in one glance.

# CHAPTER 3

## *The Confusion*

**16th May 2018**

Sam woke up with a headache the next morning. He looked at the watch. It was 11 AM. "What the Fuck. I overslept. Shit, the cook would have come and rang the bell. Let me call her and check if she can come later", he murmured.

A hangover after a late night party or getting up late was not unusual but what was bothering Sam was the face of the old man when he came across at the traffic signal last night. He was not able to take his mind off his gaze.

Those fiery, red eyes were saying something or at least trying to tell him something.

He shrugged his head in denial and told himself "What are you thinking Sam? You met a drunk guy who was possibly a thief too. How can you ponder your thoughts on something so trivial?"

It was Saturday today and Sam had no plans yet. He prepared himself some coffee, went to the balcony and sat on the chair.

Late Mornings are not so pleasant in Delhi in May as temperatures can reach up to 42-43 degrees Celsius.

Sam was recalling last night's conversation with Preeti & Rohit. “When will he grow up? I don’t understand, in which world does he live?” Sam muttered.

Sam’s apartment was on the 3rd floor in a standalone building. His apartment’s balcony opened towards an empty land. This land was usually occupied by children in mornings and evenings, but it was now 11:30 AM and the heat was scorching so no one dared to venture into the open land.

While sipping his coffee and almost half awake, from the corner of his right eye, he saw a figure lurking in the bushes of that open land. Initially, he did not give heed to it as beggars usually wander off there at night, but this man was blatantlystaring at his apartment and to be precise towards him.

Sam rubbed his eyes, put down the coffee mug and then tried to see that old man clearly and to his horror, it was the same old, thin man he saw last night at the traffic signal.

This can’t be! This is not real. “Hello, hello, who are you?”

Sam took a step back and shouted at the old man, Sam waved his hand, but the old man kept staring at him. Sam was convinced that the old man was a thief, and he had followed him here or maybe he had been following him for a long time now.

Sam's face became pale. That old man had the same gaze as last night and Sam could feel it from such a long distance. He decided to check on that guy. He finished his coffee in a single gulp, and came back to his room. Picking up aniron rod, heheaded directly to the lift. Suddenly there was a power cut and the lift stopped working. As Sam took the stairs, it took a few minutes for him to walk  to that empty land, by that time the old man had disappeared.

Sam was standing there in disbelief wondering how can someone do that? Intruding in someone's private life and that too their home.

On his way back, he dialled Rohit's mobile number.

"Hello hero, good morning. How will you save India from China if you sleep so much?" Sam said and started laughing.

"I have been awake since 8 am dude. Not like you, sleeping like a dog" Rohit said sarcastically and laughed.

"Ok, listen" Sam said, "what's your plan for the evening? If you are free, let's go to Engage. I like that place and Saturday evening is Bollywood music. Your brother will dance like Govinda today." And then Sam burst into laughter and Rohit too joined him.

It was a hot afternoon on a typical day in May. Sam took a shower and then got busy with what he liked the most, reading about the Indian Stock Market. This was a newfound interest and passion for him. But numbers are the most intoxicated objects in the world and Sam did not take a long time to find this. He soon dozed off.

A strange phenomenon followed Sam in his dreams. He found himself on a hill, near a big rock, standing and looking down the hill.

"So, you are here finally" a heavy deep voice broke the silence.

Sam turned around and saw a tall, old man, with long black hair and beard, and with the same red hot fiery piercing gaze.

"Who are you?" Sam asked. "Why have you been following me?"

"HA HA HA HA HA HA HA" That old man burst into laughter. Mad laughter rather.

"I am following you! Why will I follow you? It is you who have been following me. You are seeking me. I am the one who is sought".

Sam was now standing bewildered with his mouth wide open..

"Are you out of your mind? Sam shouted. "You have been following me. First, you suddenly came in front of my car at the traffic signal and then you followed me to my home. And you dare to tell me, I am following you. Why am I here? What do you want from me?"

That old man was smiling now. He walked up to Sam and Sam, looked straight into his eyes with the same piercing gaze Sam and whispered in his ears,

"Stop fighting Sam. It is me who you seek. I am you. You are me. We are the same. I am your journey and your destination. Break the shackles of your mind and this world, recognize me. I am thy faceless, formless, nameless who you have been seeking all your current and past lives."

"What bullshit" Sam shouted and woke up. He was sweating profusely. His face was pale. He was trying to understand what he just dreamt about. Who is that old man? What kind of sorcery is this? Is he a ghost? Ghost, this thought made him shiver in the hot afternoon of May.

It was 3 PM and it was still very hot outside. Sam looked outside from the window to see if that old man was still there.

He went out on the balcony but found no trace of that old man. He came back to his room, took a water bottle from the fridge and finished it in one go.

Sam was now confused. He was not able to understand or believe what that old man said in his dream. "I am not seeking you. You are seeking me from past lives." This was a creepy thought for him.

"What am I seeking? And why shall I seek anything from an old man, that too on a hill? If I see him again, I shall report this to the police now", He muttered.

Sam was not sleepy anymore. He switched on the TV and started watching some random videos on YouTube.

While he was browsing, he came across a weird but catchy title of a video, "Can a man fly? Can a man disappear in thin air"?

While he read the title, he thought of that old man and murmured, "That bastard can definitely disappear in thin air."

This video was a documentary made by a tourist from Bangalore in year 2000. It was a 60-minute video. What surprised Sam was this old video which had appeared in his feed eventhough he never watched such stuff on YouTube.

"Ok, I have 2 hours to leave home before I meet Rohit. Let me watch this dumb shit." He told himself.

In this documentary, a student named Akash travels to Badrinath from Bangalore. Badrinath is a famous pilgrimage site in India. It is located in the Himalayas region in Uttarakhand state in North India.

Badrinath temple is visited by millions from India & abroad every year to seek blessings from Lord Shiva.

Aakash also travelled to Badrinath to seek Shiva's blessing. It was December 2000. Aakash was travelling with his college group. There were 4 in total.

The route to Badrinath is not so simple or straight. They took a train to reach New Delhi and from there they boarded a bus for Dehradun, another hill town in the Uttarakhand state. From Dehradun, they boarded a taxi to reach Badrinath.

10 km before Badrinath, they encountered a landslide, and their taxi could not go further so they had to deboard and decided to cover the rest of the distance by foot.

The group embarked on their journey by foot in the hilly terrain unknown to them. The track was treacherous, with no signboard, foggy and no sight of any animal or human.

It was 4 pm and the sun was nowhere to be seen. It was busy playing hide-n-seek with clouds. Chilly winds had made the track even more difficult and none in the group had ever put their feet on snow before let alone walking.

Aakash was the youngest in the group. He had never witnessed a snowfall in his life so he was very thrilled to see snowfall for the first time in his life. He was making snowballs and throwing them onto his friends. The group was having fun.

They had barely walked 2 KM so far when they found themselves in trouble. A landslide had taken away a part of the track and now there was a 20 feet-wide gap in the road and god knows how deep the gap was.

They were in real trouble now. It was 5 PM, and there was nowhere to go. Going back was not an option.

Saurabh, the eldest of them all, suddenly started shouting at Sai. "It was your idea to take this route." Because of you, now, we are all in trouble".

"Have you gone crazy? Sai retorted, "We could not have gone back. You only asked what do we do now. So, I suggested, let's go on foot. You were very excited then and now you are blaming me. What the fuck man!"

"Hold on, guys. Why are we fighting? We are in this together." Aakash intervened, "We all had decided to come on a trip together so whatever happens here, we all have to take responsibility and stay as a group in every condition. Right now, we have to find a way to move to the other side rather than digging our graves here."

Sai nodded in agreement and gave a "Fuck you" look to Saurabh who was looking down the ditch.

“Can we create a bridge across that point?” Sai proposed, “We can find a long wooden log and place it across and cross over it walking”.

But where shall we find such a long wooden log Mr. Always right?” Saurabh said sarcastically.

“We can use you as a log, but you are a bit short,” Sai said, and everyone started laughing.

Sun had already bid goodbye and night was spreading its wings around them. It was already very cold and getting colder with every minute going by. There was no solution in sight.

None of them had ever experienced such weather before and they were at the mercy of nature now. They were in a forest full of wild animals and complete darkness, with wind speed up to 50km/hour, temperature below 0 already, a deep ditch in front of them and no road to go back, they were in for serious trouble ahead.

They were all shivering. The food supply was dwindling with only two bottles of water remaining. They had not anticipated this even in their worst dreams.

“Sai, you always watch the Discovery channel a lot. They show you how to survive such a situation. This is the time you make the discovery channel founder proud.” Saurabh asked Sai mockingly.

Sai gave a morbid look to Saurabh and looked up and said, “We need help from there”.

Mohit, who was silent all this time, started crying. “We shall all die here. What have I seen in my life so far? The first time I ventured out of my home, I met you guys and now I will die here. Oh Lord Shiva, I am your follower, please save me from your wrath. What have I done to get this punishment? I know for sure, Saurabh drinks beer in his room when alone, so please take him but spare my life.”

Saurabh who was already at the receiving end of this group, lost his cool now. “You moron. Why should I die? You should die in fact. Lord Shiva, I must tell you, this pseudo-follower, has pictures of naked ladies on his computer and that is what he worships all the time. What has the world come to now? People want others to die for their own sins. I strongly think we should throw you in this ditch and Lord Shiva may become happy with our sacrifice and help us reach the other side.”

Nobody laughed this time. Extreme cold had taken their senses away. It was pitch dark everywhere. Clueless as they were, the night had no restraint, no mercy to shower. All 4 of them are sitting close to each other, holding each other now.

Suddenly they heard a noise, the ringing of a bell. This noise was not coming from very far off the location they were, and this was becoming clearer and louder with each second. They were all terrified but were not able to move from that place.

"What could it be?" Saurabh asked,

"I think it's a cow," Sai replied.

"Can you talk sense sometimes?" Saurabh angrily said.

"I think it is a tiger", Mohit said.

"Hello, you dumbass, Saurabh said, "Which tiger has a bell around its neck? And shut the fuck up or else I will feed you to that Tiger."

Mohit, the poor guy, who was also regretting his decision to come here, was completely convinced it was his last day.

"Can you all just stay silent for a while?" Sai said, "This voice is getting closer and closer. Let us just stay together, wait and watch" Everyone nodded.

Meanwhile, Saurabh and Aakash picked up a stone each in their hands.

"What is this?" Sai asked.

"This is for our defence in case the tiger attacks." Aakash replied.

Sai sighed and started looking towards the point where that noise was coming from.

Someone was walking towards them.

"Oh No, robbers," Saurabh screamed.

"Shut up moron", Sai said and put his hand on Saurabh's mouth.

"Oh Lord Shiva, first landslide, then snow and now a robber. What do you want? If I can escape safely from the clutches of certain death and misery, I will offer prasadam for 21 Rupees."

Mohit said, almost crying. Everyone looked at Mohit and laughed sheepishly.

"You owe me 10 Rupees by the way," Aakash said to Mohit.

"Come on guys, can we please focus? If we survive this, I shall give 21 Rupees to each of you as a token of thanks" Sai said.

"You also owe me 10 Rupees" Aakash said sarcastically to Sai.

"Who is there?" A loud but deep voice broke their post-survival financial discussion.

They saw a tall, white-bearded, old man standing in front of them.

"Who are you, people? What are you doing here?"

"Who, who, the, the, the fuck, fuck fuck, are you? Saurabh asked stammering and in a meek voice.

"I am the keeper of this place. But how did you get here? Where do you want to go?"

“We are stuck here, Babaji. We are travelling to Badrinath and on the way, due to a landslide, we decided to travel the rest of the distance by foot. But we had no idea about the place and weather conditions. There is a big and deep ditch ahead, which we can not cross, and we cannot go back either, So we are stuck here”, Sai said in one breath.

“Mohit held Saurabh's arm and whispered in his ear, “Why this ass Sai is trying to act smart and telling that old man everything. He will rob us of our belongings and leave us here to die.”

“'You have a pair of underwear and two shirts in that bag. And do you think that old man will need any of that stinking garbage?”, Saurabh whispered back.

Mohit left his arm, looked at him angrily and started looking at the old man, who was observing all of them.

He was wearing a thin linen cloth wrapped around his waist, no slippers or shoes, open hair, but no sign of weather taking a toll on him. It seemed as if he was part of that nature and emerged out of it. He had a striking gaze, and his eyes were fiery red, so sharp that the pitch-dark night could not hide them. His voice was like the thunder of the striking light. He was standing unfazed by chilly weather, snow and wind in his one small piece of linen cloth and half naked while others were shivering in their woollen jackets.

"Come, follow me. I shall show you the path and help you pass that ditch" That old man said and moved forward.

All of them followed him like a herd of sheep. They were all mesmerised by him now and devoid of any option now.

"Why is he not feeling cold?"Saurabh asked.

"Keep your mouth shut and follow him or else I will throw you in that ditch", Aakash said Angrily.

Mohit was holding both his hands in prayer posture and walking. "Lord Shiva, you finally listened to my prayer" He muttered.

That old man stopped near the beginning of that ditch. He bent forward and looked down as if he was trying to measure the depth. He then turned towards the group, closed his eyes and stood a standstill. All four of them looked at each other and started wondering what next.

"Bro, this guy is high on weed. I don't think he can help us. But if he has some weed, it can certainly help us indeed", Aakash said sheepishly.

Sai hit him on his head from behind and said, "If I Survive this, trust me, the first thing I will do is kill you".

"So you want him to survive, so that you can kill him later. What kind of survival is this?" Saurabh said and started laughing.

“Come here, all of you”, that old man asked them to come near him.

He asked them to close their eyes and held each other's hands.

“Why should we close our eyes?”, Sai asked that old man.

“If you want to cross to the other side, you will have to trust me. If you want to die here, I am ok to leave you”. The old man said.

all 4 of them looked at each other puzzled. “What do we do? Will he push us into this ditch and we all shall die? He asked us to hold hands so that he ensured none of us survives and no evidence is left and then he can rob our belongings.” Mohit said this to the group.

“We have no option but to believe him. I do not know but there is no other option. All of us will carry our backpacks with us and then will hold hands, so that he can not get anything even if he pushes us into the ditch.” Sai suggested.

“We don’t have the whole night,” the old man shouted.

They all held each other's hands and closed their eyes. Sai was leading the group. The old man held Sai’s hand and started walking.

“May what happens, do not open your eyes!” The old man warned them.

They started walking towards the ditch with their eyes closed. Mohit opened his right eye partially and saw them moving towards the ditch.

He murmured to the group, "Hey guys, he is leading us towards the ditch."

"Mohit, you asshole! Close your eyes man" Sai said angrily.

"No, he has a point. Why are we following that old man like an idiot? This does not seem like help." Saurabh said.

Before anyone could say anything, they felt a sudden warmth around them. Their eyes were closed but they could feel the light around them, curious they were, they opened their eyes and what they saw next, their eyes could not believe it.

That half-naked barefoot old man was glowing like a ball of fire. Like thousands of bulbs were lit suddenly.

Sai was still holding his hand and all of them were still moving towards the ditch. They were all numb now, mouths and eyes wide open, following that old man like an inebriated man does for a glass of whiskey.

He set his foot in the air to cross the ditch as if there was a bridge. And what they all saw next, they thought it as a dream, as an illusion.

He was walking in the air. Sai was right behind him and he looked at that old man as if he had seen a ghost. Mohit was behind Sai and he was trembling and looking down and chanting Shiva's mantra. Aakash was following Mohit, and he was as bewildered as others. And the last one, Saurabh, started to cry out of fear.

It took them all 30 seconds to cross that pit and the moment they reached the other side, that old man turned around and for the first time they saw his face clearly.

They thought he was an old man, but he looked no older than 20 years. He was smiling at them. His eyes were fiery red, his gaze could pierce into their souls. Sai could feel a strong connection. His wandering mind suddenly stopped, and he could see that man looking straight into his eyes. In fact, all of them could feel him looking straight into their eyes.

They were not able to move or feel their body. The only thing they could see was his eyes, which had taken away all chattering of their mind and their thoughts. They were all standing there still.

That man suddenly stepped back, laughed and said, "You were seeking me, so I brought you here, You were not here by chance. Your destiny led to me."

He had a hearty laugh and he again started glowing like a ball of fire. All four of them could not tolerate that gaze and light and closed their eyes.

When they opened their eyes, that man had disappeared in thin air.

***

"What the fuck?" Sam muttered, "People will post anything to get views and likes. The bastard wasted my time. Oh, it is 4:30 already. I need to get ready." Sam got up and started to get ready.

# CHAPTER 4

## *The Conversation*

13th November 2008

"So, Samrat, what's your story? By the way, I like your name, Samrat, like a king. Where is your Kingdom, dude? Oops, I mean Samrat?" Akshay asked jokingly.

"In my ass!", Samrat said laughing,

"And my story! Dude, I am a fucked-up HR slogging my ass for 10 hours for Rupees 25000 every month. This is my story", Samrat replied and started laughing.

Akshay looked at him and asked, "Can I call you Sam? That sounds much better but only if Shri Shri 1008 great Samrat allows us peasants to do so?", Akshay asked, teasing him.

"Sam indeed sounds better. My friends used to call me Sam in college, so yes, Sam is cool ", Samrat replied.

"Ok and can I ask you something if you don't mind?", Akshay asked.

"Sure, go ahead", Sam replied.

"What do you want to do in life, I mean, what kind of job would you like to do", Akshay asked.

Sam thought for a while and replied, "Your brother would love to be an entrepreneur someday and run his own company and fuck everyone like everyone fucks him right now". Both started laughing.

Akshay then put his right hand around his shoulder and said 'cheers'. They both took a large sip of their whiskey.

"I also want to start my own business, but this job and my girlfriend just do not give me enough time to think and work on it", Akshay said with a deep voice and started looking at pretty girls seated right in front of them.

"ooooo, so you have a girlfriend, aha, lucky dude", Sam winked at Akshay and started looking in the same direction where those pretty girls were seated.

"Asshole, that's not the point. I said, I also want to start my own business", Akshay said looking at Sam.

"Come on dude, look at those beauties there, we can always start our business after this. Right now, all we need is Vitamin See and that is right there. You need motivation in life to do something and there is so much motivation here", Sam said and started laughing. Akshay looked at him and said, "Moron" and he too started laughing.

"Ok, so do you have any idea? I have none", Sam asked Akshay.

"Actually, I have one idea and I discussed it with some people, but none took me seriously".

"What is that? Tell me", Sam said.

"So, I think, India lacks a lot of trained people in terms of communication skills and this is a billion-dollar opportunity. I also know, there are already a lot of people in the market working on this but if we provide a full package to educational institutions, we can make it big", Akshay explained.

"But there are already a lot of trained professionals and firms tapping this opportunity and how do you plan to differentiate yourself from them?", Sam asked.

"As I said, we need to prepare a package, something, which is not just soft skills but also includes analytical skills. We need to focus on employability, rather than just plain training", Akshay replied.

"This makes sense. I had a similar thought but then I saw too much competition in this segment so shrugged off the thought. But now, you are also saying the same thing, I think, We can discuss it more.", Sam said.

"Sounds like a plan. Cheers my friend, Let's order one more large peg", Akshay said with excitement in his voice.

That day, Sam did not feel empty sitting in that Bar. It felt meaningful to him. First time in his life, he was discussing a subject he felt closest to the most. He was elated.

"Let us do one thing. There is a coffee shop around the corner. It is usually empty. Let's meet there daily after office or whenever we can. And I am serious. I don't know if it will work or not, but we should discuss it at least", Sam proposed.

"Cool. So, now we have an agenda and a place. Can I also bring my girlfriend along? This is actually her idea and I don't want her to think I stole her billion dollars", Akshay said and started laughing.

"More the merrier", Sam said "We definitely need more people and ideas and as much help as we can".

They both stayed for some more time and surprisingly, Sam stayed silent all this while. He felt light and peaceful after a long time and the first time he realised that one of the bartenders was a girl.

"Looks like my eyes really opened today", Sam said to himself. Akshay too was enjoying the music and his drink. Soon they both bid goodnight to each other and left for their homes.

Sam walked to the nearby Metro station. It was 11:30 PM and the last metro for the day was on its way in 3 minutes. Sam had been thinking about the conversation. "Entrepreneur, own boss, Wow, sounds so cool. Once I open my business, I shall show my middle finger to Sharma and won't even serve notice period and resign. Just a few months, and I shall purchase a good car. Enough of this metro business. It is getting crowded. I will be a businessman soon". Sam was talking to himself and this thought made him feel very different.

He suddenly took his jacket in his hand and laptop bag in another hand.

"I need to start grooming myself. May be, should start buying new clothes. And I definitely need a new laptop bag. This looks so college type. Entrepreneurs have an aura, a style and a personality and I need to have all that", Sam was in his thoughts and in a different world.

All of a sudden, the metro entered the station and Sam's castle of thoughts broke at once. He boarded the metro, reached home, changed his clothes and crashed in his bed. Soon, he was in the tight grip of sleep but this time it brought along the dreams of business, entrepreneurship and showing middle finger to Sharma.

# CHAPTER 5

## *The Flashback*

**16$^{th}$ May 2018**

Sam got ready and left to meet Rohit. It was 6:30 PM and still very bright. Days are hot and long in summers in India. The plan was to meet in Starbucks in Orion Mall and from there head to Engage together.

Sam directly headed to Starbucks but on the way, he suddenly stopped to have a look at his favourite place, Crossword. Bookstores were Sam's weakness. If he chances upon a bookstore amidst any work or place, like a child, he will simply be lost in the world of fairytales, memories, stories and conversation.

Sam walked straight into Crossword, the bookstore, just to have a look around. He was always mesmerised by the smell of the new books, its colour and the images on the cover.

While he was lost in his world, he saw a book with black cover, not easily visible as it was lying in the leftmost corner of the last bookshelf. He was surprised to find that book in the children section which seemed like a novel. "What are you doing here, you black beauty?", he looked at the book and murmured.

When he picked the book, he was in for a rude shock. There was a face on the cover of the book which seemed familiar to him. It resembled the old man who he had been seeing for the last 2 days.

An old man with wrinkled face, red & fiery eyes and the title of the book said, "The Unknown".

He started laughing, "Dude, this old man must be something. Already a celebrity he is, Sam told himself. That book was written by someone named Sai Kiran.

"oh, so two people have written this book, Sai & Kiran, must be his wife I think", He said mockingly while looking at the cover. He was at his sarcastic best. And this old man must be their grandfather".

He opened the book and flipped a few pages. Nothing interesting he found. He then looked at the last few pages to know more about the author Sai Kiran.

"About the author, what about you Sai & Kiran? Oh, you are from Bangalore and this book is based on a true story and personal experiences of four friends who during an expedition to Badrinath Dham ", Sam suddenly stopped while reading and his eyes opened wide and suddenly changed from just glancing to reading and the voice went up in volume, just like a Lamborghini car goes from 0 to 100 km in 3 seconds. His gaze just stuck on the last line, which read and completed the above sentence, “Met a strange phenomenon which cannot be explained”.

“Oye hero, what are you doing here?”, Rohit came from behind and tapped on Sam’s shoulder. “Your phone is not reachable either.”

“And you read children’s books!” Rohit said mockingly and burst in laughter. This sudden entry of Rohit brought Sam out of whatever trance he was in.

“I was just having a look at some of these books here”, Sam said. “It's 7 pm already. Let’s go to engage. Happy hours will end at 8 pm”, Rohit said, and Sam just followed him.

Engage is an amazing place with an electrifying atmosphere. The crowd is young and vibrant. Sam loved this place, and this has been his one of the favourite places in Delhi.

There is a certain corner in the lounge, which was his usual place to sit. But that corner was not available today, a group of 3 pretty girls had already occupied it. Sam looked at them and said in a sad childish tone, “Oh No, my fortress has fallen. Where will we sit now?”.

“Hello sir! May I help you? How many of you are here?” One of the lounge staff came to them and asked.

“Oh, we are just two of us”, Rohit replied.

That staff guy pointed towards a table which was empty and they both headed towards it. That table was right opposite to his favourite corner where those three pretty girls were seated.

Sam ordered his usual double black whiskey and Rohit ordered a beer.

"You see those girls, in that corner", Rohit asked Sam, "That one in Red is just mind-blowing".

"Why do you act like an internet explorer sometimes?", Sam asked Rohit.

"What do you mean by Internet Explorer?",Rohit asked looking in that corner.

"Dumbass, I saw them already and that girl in red smiled at me when we entered", Sam said, winking at Rohit.

Rohit burst into laughter and said, "What are you high on? Which weed have you been smoking? Isn't it a little early to start it?"

Sam ignored Rohit and started to look around.

"Ok listen, I need to tell you something" Sam said to Rohit, "But then you have to believe me. I know, I was drunk last night but when I am going to tell you, I experienced it in my full consciousness."

"I cannot guarantee If I can believe you. And if you are going to tell me a crazy story, then I shall certainly believe you have been smoking weed. And, by the way, you promised to dance like Govinda today. You promised in the morning over call", Rohit said and started laughing again.

"Go fuck yourself then. I won't tell anything", Sam said irritatingly.

"Ok, blabber, whatever you have to", Rohit said looking at that table.

"You desperate pervert, look at me, not there", Sam said.

"Are you going to dance or what? I need ears, not eyes to listen, and why shall I look at you here when I can look at beautiful faces around me? And will you start or need me to sit in your lap?" Rohit said amusingly.

"Ok, so here we go. A disclaimer, all this happened in the last 2 days and is still happening and I may be overthinking so just wanted to validate if I am crazy" Sam said.

"You do not need validation. You are a certified dumb fuck" Rohit said and started laughing.

"Huh, listen now", Sam started narrating the incident, "So, last night, while I was driving back, I stopped at a traffic signal. Suddenly an old man appeared In Front of me. I first mistook him for a beggar, but he had been staring at me and had a striking gaze. So, I thought he must be a drunkard or high on weed. And then, I went home and slept. In the morning...",

Rohit interrupted him and said laughing, "Did he chase you to your apartment and fuck you?

"You fucker! Shut your mouth and listen", Sam Said irritatingly.

"If you interrupt again, I shall hit you hard this time.

Rohit made a zip sign on his lips and pretended to be a serious listener.

"Ok, so in the morning, while I was having coffee sitting on the balcony, I saw the same old man in the empty land opposite my flat. I first thought, It must be a different guy but this guy had the same gaze, the same eyes which I can never forget. And then I saw the same old man in my dreams, and he was talking about some destiny. I am seeking him and some bullshit."

"So, dude, I am sorry to hear that you have to see old men in your dreams these days. I always had my doubts. Did you two make love?", Rohit said in a serious tone and took a big sip from his beer.

"Will you please shut the fuck up?" Sam said angrily.

"Only fuck, no shut up"," Rohit said smiling.

"Listen you bastard", Sam was visibly irritated now.

"So, in the morning when I went to that empty land, he was already gone as if he was never there. But this is not the most surprising part".

Rohit interrupted Sam again, "Did he remind you of the dream and ask for the incomplete love-making session? He burst into laughter and this time;

Sam also had a smile on his face. "Dude, you are not taking me seriously. After we spoke about meeting in the evening, I was browsing some YouTube videos and I came across this creepy video with a lunatic title, 'Can a man walk in the air? Can a man disappear in thin air', something like that, because I was disturbed by that morning incident and god knows what came over me, I started watching that video. It was a bloody one-hour documentary. Can you believe that Sam, your Sam can watch something like that?" Sam stopped while narrating.

"You have been enlightening me for 20 minutes now and I am starting to believe also. By the way, where did you get that weed that made you so high? Did that old man provide it? Do not hide it from me, you fucker" Rohit teased Sam.

"Suck my dick and you will be high too", Sam said and winked at Rohit.

"So, that is what is keeping you busy these days, wow. Asking people to suck your dick", Rohit laughed so hard, he almost fell from the chair and some whiskey splattered from his mouth.

"You are right. So in that documentary...", Sam continued the narration not caring or giving any fuck to whatever Rohit had said.

"In that video, a group of four students from south India travel to Badrinath. There was a landslide on the way, and to complete the rest of the distance, they chose to go barefoot. They took a trail through a forest area. On their way, they saw the road was caved in due to a landslide and there was nowhere to go. They waited for some time, but no one came. After some time, an old man appeared from nowhere and offered help".

"Are you listening, to what I am saying?" Sam stopped to check if Rohit was paying attention.

"How can I not listen? This is so damn interesting. I am also interested in that girl in red, I mean old man", Rohit replied looking at the corner table.

Sam turned around to see in that corner. The girl in the red dress from that group was having a smoke.

"Fucker, I see what you are interested in", Sam said to Rohit.

"I am interested in that old man, my friend. Just me and that old man, in the snow, dancing around, having smoke, drinking", Rohit said slowly in a soft voice taking a small sip of his whiskey, eyes half closed.

Sam hit Rohit on the left shoulder with his hand and said, "This was not an orgy video, you fucker. Let me complete, or else I will knock you off."

"For old man, please wrap up fast" Rohit folded his hand and said in a mocking voice.

"So, that old man asked those four students to hold each other's hand and close their eyes. He then held the hand of the first guy. He suddenly started to glow like a giant fireball and was levitating including all four of them. He took them through the caved-in road which was actually a big ditch. And once they crossed that ditch, he disappeared in thin air and then the video ends, and by the way, it was not an old man, but a young boy in his mid-twenties but he had the same gaze, same eyes and he spoke of same destiny and seeker stuff which I saw in my dream. And today, while you met me in Crossword, I saw a book which had the same old man, with the same gaze, same eyes. I am now wondering, is this some kind of a joke, some message or some voodoo shit"

"By the way, you mentioned a young boy in that video. First, an old man, then a young boy. Did you not meet any lady till now? My suggestion is to wait for some days, and you might see a sexy lady too and that will be real fun. It's all just a build-up for a real adventure my friend, "Rohit said teasing Sam,

"And my adventure is coming to this side. Oh god, she is already shining like fire. If you see that old man in dreams again, please ask him to give me some whoop ass superpower".

Sam held his face in his arms and said to himself, "I shall ask that old man to give you a shiny dick on the head". He took a big sip of the whiskey, unlocked his mobile, opened Instagram and started looking at the random reels.

Sam was not able to take his mind off the face of that old man and his gaze.

"I will be back from the restroom", he said to Rohit and left. But he headed outside the lounge and went directly towards the crossword bookstore. He went straight to the children's section and tried to find that book. But it was nowhere to be found. He started to look for it in all sections, but it had simply disappeared like that old man did in thin air.

Suddenly, his phone rang.

"Where are you? Which restroom did you go, fucker? Don't tell me you are shitting there", Rohit said.

"I got a call, so I came out. I will see you in 5 minutes", Sam replied.

Sam was wondering, where did the book go? It was there hardly an hour back. He went to the billing counter and inquired about the book.

"There was a book in the children's section, I think it's title was 'Unknown', written by uumm, I guess some Sai Kiran. Could you please check if you have that in the store?"

"Sure sir", the guy at the billing counter said. He took a few seconds and replied, "There was just one copy of that book with us, and it got sold today, around half an hour back."

"oh ok. No problem. Thanks a lot for your help", Sam thanked the guy at the counter and headed back to the lounge where he found Rohit at the opposite table with those three pretty girls, talking to them.

"Hey, here is the man. Meet Sam, my friend, my brother from another mother", Rohit introduced him to those girls.

"Hi Sam, I am Rishika", the girl in the Red dress introduced herself.

"Hey, Sam here. Nice meeting you", Sam smiled at her.

Sam held Rohit's arm, took him a few feet distance away and whispered in his ears, "You fucker, you had been drooling at her. Finally, you got to talk to her".

"Asshole, where were you all this while?", Rohit asked amusingly, "I did this for you only. Afterall, I am your best friend." Rohit said and started smiling.

Sam was there, this was his typical lifestyle, but he was not there mentally. "Ok, ok, So, what is the plan now? Do we sit with them or what?", Sam asked Rohit.

"Of course, dumbass. let's go to them now else they might start thinking we are gays", Rohit said and walked up to those girls.

Sam did not follow him but stood still for a while.

"Why am I not able to enjoy all this? What is wrong with me? What is happening? Why is my mind drifting?

Why the fuck have I been thinking of that old man? I know, it is not the man but all these strange events which are making me feel weird", Sam's mind was abuzz with these thoughts and questions.

Sam joined those girls with Rohit at their table. He was unusually silent, and Rohit could very well notice it. He asked him, "What's wrong with you? You have been weird since we came here. Is it that old man episode that's bothering you? Sam, this is life. See around. We work hard to enjoy and live this kind of life and you are thinking about some lunatic. Come on dude".

"No, nothing like it. I do not know. It's not my day it looks like. But you guys carry on. I will finish my drink and might go back home early", Sam said.

"What the fuck dude? Are you crazy or what? Relax, have one more drink and you will feel better", Rohit tried to cheer him up.

Sam just nodded his head and started looking outside. This lounge was on the 10th floor of a commercial building, and he could see the play of lights outside. Traffic was alive and everyone seemed to be in a hurry to reach their destination.

Sam was restless. He was 2 drinks down, but he did not seem to enjoy anything today. Suddenly, he got up and went out into the open area, which was actually a smoking zone.

"Excuse me guys, I will just be right back", Sam said to the group and left.

It was hot and humid outside, and the smell of smoke was filling his lungs. He stood near the railings and started looking down.

"Where is everyone going? Do all reach their destination on time or do they ever reach? What is everyone seeking? Money, job, fame, girlfriend, wife, kids, career, house, car or what? What am I seeking? I have everything I wanted at this stage of life. Good friends, money, a good job, a house. After whatever happened in 2015, I think, I came a long way".

After a long time, Sam was introspecting. Whenever he drinks, he either starts singing or gets silent but today was different. He was traversing the memories of his past. A past, which made him Sam from Samrat.

Sam got divorced in 2015. The end of his relationship with his wife became murky at the end and divorce added a sour taste to it. Sam lost everything in that divorce, all his life savings, his house, all belongings, all that he ever possessed and even had to take a huge personal loan. The only thing he was left with was his job, his trove of books which he always considered his soul, a newfound freedom and peace of mind.

The recollection of bitter memories, betrayal and suffering brought tears to Sam's eyes. He wiped his eyes, sighed deeply and took a sip from his whiskey glass.

Suddenly, he felt a soft touch on his shoulders. It was Rohit. They both have been good friends for ten years now and Rohit could always figure out whenever Sam got into a shell and became silent.

He could always recognize the real Samrat behind that mask of flamboyance, smile, playboy and high-on-life guy. So, Rohit could figure out something was amiss.

"Thinking of her?", Rohit asked.

"Not exactly, just contemplating on life", Sam replied.

"I also want to meet that old man now. He must be some influence", Rohit said wondering, "By the way, if you want, we can leave early. I am absolutely ok with that. But how can you leave the company of those beautiful girls, man?", Rohit said laughing.

Sam smiled, looked at Rohit and said, "It is one of those days when you don't know what to expect or do. Sometimes, we should just be in the moment and take some time to reflect. Some events bring back the memories of the past and haunt our present. It is one of those days and I don't know what to do", Sam said with a heaviness in his voice.

“I think I will leave you in the company of those girls. You will be happy anyways, I know. You are allowed to enjoy at least one day without me”, Sam said and started laughing.

Then, I shall also come”, Rohit said.

“No, no, it’s alright. I am in a different mood altogether. You stay. I will call you tomorrow. And don’t worry, I will be just fine. I just need some alone time with me”, Sam said and hugged Rohit and left. On his way back, he went to those girls, apologised for leaving early and said goodbye.

# CHAPTER 6

## The Middle Finger

**November 2008 onwards**

Sam and Akshay became good friends and started meeting regularly in the office. They both kept busy at work, so they did not get a chance to discuss the business idea that Akshay had proposed.

It had been a month since they both went to DROP. On a Friday evening, Sam saw Akshay waiting for the lift.

"Hey dude, what's happening?", Sam tapped Akshay's shoulder from behind.

"Hey Hi. Where are you Samrat of no Kingdom? You just disappeared."

"Where will I go? Sharma will not let me go anywhere.", Sam sighed and continued, "What happened to our business idea? I was waiting to hear from you."

"Good question", Akshay said and started thinking. "Let's meet tomorrow in Noida sector 18 if you are free. There is a cafe coffee day. Me and Ruchi go there frequently".

"Ruchi who? Your girlfriend?", Sam asked.

"Oh, yes. Ruchi is my girlfriend. I think I told you", Akshay replied.

"Yes. You said she will also come along when we meet to discuss the business idea", Sam said.

"Yup, I think, I told you, it's her business idea so she can explain it better. And anyway, she is serving a notice period. Her company is laying off employees", Akshay said in a worried tone.

"Oh. That must be very stressful. I can understand. We also had to ask many employees to leave last month due to poor performance in our business region. I am afraid one day Sharma may also ask me to leave", Sam said and continued, "So, let us meet tomorrow. About what time", Sam asked.

"How about evening around 5PM?", Akshay asked.

"Cool with me. Let's meet tomorrow then", Sam said and they both said goodbye to each other and left.

***

Sam was excited about this meeting. Afterall, he had contemplated all his life to start his business venture, and this is exactly what he wanted. First time since he arrived in Delhi, he felt he was doing something meaningful on a Saturday.

He reached the cafe coffee day at 4:30 PM, 30 minutes earlier than what Akshay had proposed. He ordered his favourite cappuccino coffee. He had brought his laptop along as he thought Akshay and his girlfriend might want to share any document or a presentation. He opened his laptop and started browsing some random documents.

"Look, who is here already", Akshay came from behind and tapped Sam's shoulders. "You are early, dude", Akshay said.

"I was bored at home so thought of starting early", Sam said.

"That's cool. Ok, meet Ruchi, the future Billionaire and, here is Samrat, the king of no Kingdom. You can call him Sam though", Sam introduced them and started laughing.

"Do we need a laptop?", Akshay looked at Sam's laptop and asked.

"Oh, was I supposed to prepare a presentation for this meeting?", Ruchi asked, wondering.

"No, no. I brought this laptop thinking if you plan to share anything. Never mind, it's just a habit. I carry my laptop all the time with me. It's my escape from boredom", Sam replied with a smile.

"Then it's alright but don't worry. We won't let you get bored", Ruchi said smiling.

Ruchi asked Sam about his native place, his educational background and his inclination towards the business. Sam was more than happy to answer all the questions. It was more of knowing each other. He got to know, Ruchi & Akshay have been together since their MBA days. He also felt sad about Ruchi's laying off from her job, he did not speak about it though and pretended as if he knew nothing.

Sam had an instant liking for both of them. It was also an instant connection. They sat in the CCD till 9 PM. They discussed a lot of things, right from business models to investment, partnership, challenges, taking out time from jobs and whatnot.

While returning home, Sam was delighted and felt at peace. This is the kind of discussion he always wanted to have. He told himself, "If nothing else works out, I shall gain two good friends".

***

They started meeting almost daily\ in another coffee shop near the office.

After deliberation for many days, they agreed on the name for their first venture "Global Skills Training Group".

"GST Group. I like this name. One day, it will be shining on a neon board on a tall building in Delhi. All floors will belong to us. One will be able to see this building from a distance", Sam shouted like a kid.

"AMEN", Said Ruchi & Akshay together.

"Ok, so we have a name and now we need to get the company registered and open a bank account", Ruchi said.

"Bank account is the most important. I cannot wait to get those millions", Sam said and started laughing.

"You greedy bugger. One step at a time", Akshay said smiling. "I know a Chartered Accountant who can help us. I shall speak to him and let you know both the next steps", Akshay said.

"Cool. I need to push off. Sharma had asked for a report by tonight, so I need to finish it. See you guys tomorrow", Sam said and left. Akshay & Ruchi also left after a while.

***

The trio kept meeting in that cafe. Akshay managed to speak with the chartered accountant and was able to register the company and open a bank account too. The dream which they had seen was taking shape slowly. Sam was very excited. It was the beginning of a new journey and new challenges were lying ahead. But, right now, they were basking in the glory of whatever little they had achieved, unaware of the devils of the unknown future.

# CHAPTER 7

## *The Start*

**November 2008 onwards**

Sam had just reached the office. His boss called him into his cabin. Sam thought it's gonna be a usual bashing as he was late as usual. He had not even opened his laptop.

He looked at Meera who was sitting right in front of him. She winked at him and said, "Good luck! Though you don't need it but still" and laughed.

Sam gave her a disgusted look and went straight to his boss's cabin.

"Hey Sam! Come. How are you?", Pradeep asked him.

Sam was not ready for this sweet gesture. He was expecting the usual dialogue where Pradeep takes Sam for a ride and bashes him right, left and centre.

"Excuse me!" Sam asked.

Sam thought he may not have heard Pradeep well, so he asked, "I am sorry Pradeep. What did you say?".

Pradeep laughed hard. "How are you Sam?" he asked.

"It's fine. Going on. You know very well how it is", Sam replied sarcastically.

"Hmmm", Pradeep hummed and gave Sam a serious look.

"Listen! I want to talk to you about something very important", Pradeep said.

"What is it about?", Sam asked.

"What are your career plans?", Pradeep asked.

"You said you wanted to talk about something very important", Sam said smiling.

"So isn't your career important to you?", Pradeep asked in a serious tone.

"I am still trying to figure out my life sir. It is my first job and I have no clue how things will be tomorrow, but yes, I am learning each day", Sam said without a pause.

"Good. So let me come straight to the point now. Sam you know already, the competition in the market is too much and survival is very difficult for even seasoned players like us", Pradeep said.

"I know sir. I saw our last quarter's result. We are legging in the industry and behind almost all major players", Sam mentioned.

“Exactly, and the company is looking for ways to cut costs and reduce expenses wherever we can”, Pradeep now became more serious while he said this.

“Are you firing me?”, Sam asked, chuckling.

“I did not say this Sam”, Pradeep clarified.

“But yes, there is some restructuring plan mandate which has come from the senior management and all departments have to submit their proposals in two weeks. And you are not the only one I am talking to. This conversation is going to happen with everyone. So before I make a decision, I want everyone to be informed about why and what of it”.

“So people will lose their jobs, you mean?”, Sam asked.

“It is a possibility and we are exploring other options too. But we shall evaluate and assess and then will determine what to do. We don’t want to ask anyone to leave but if it comes to that, we shall have to. ” Pradeep said looking at his laptop screen.

“Ok, thank you for letting me know Sir”, Sam said looking outside the cabin where Meera was staring at him and trying to gaugewhat was going on inside. People had always seen Pradeep shouting at Sam, but this sight was music to their ears.

“Do you have any questions?”, Pradeep asked.

“No sir. I have no questions right now but can I ask you something apart from this, if you don’t mind?”, Sam asked.

“Oh of course”, Pradeep said.

“Should I start looking for a job outside?”, Sam asked directly.

“Sam, I did not say you will lose your job but if you find better prospects outside and if you think this is what you want to do, I won’t stop you either. But right now, you don’t have to worry. Nothing is confirmed yet”, Pradeep sighed while replying.

“Thank you sir”, Sam said and stood up and came out of the cabin. He did not go to his desk but went to the washroom.

Sam looked at himself in the mirror and kept staring at his reflection.

“So this is it? This is the end. I always knew it. I was not cut for this anyways. Bloody baldy, so much sugar in his voice. I already feel diabetic”, Sam said and pounced his fist at the mirror.

# CHAPTER 8

## *Birth of a Dream*

**November 2008 onwards**

After office, as usual, Sam met Akshay and Ruchi. He announced his decision to quit his job and focus completely on the business.

"Are you sure?", Ruchi asked.

"1000% sure. I can't stay there anymore. I know what that moron is up to. So it's better I quit before he asks me to. And now I also know where life is heading. I want to give everything to this business now. It is my dream", Sam said, sipping his tea.

Akshay was silent and had been looking at Sam all this time.

"So Sam, are you saying our jobs are not safe? I can also be asked to leave. Is it", Akshay asked worryingly.

"Dude, first of all, I don't know anything. And now you also started. Pradeep said in 2 weeks they have to submit a proposal so god knows what he is up to. And this business is our plan B. isn't it?" Sam said.

"Yeah, but there should be some backup plan right? You will quit your job and Ruchi also is not employed right now. So I don't think quitting your job is the right thing to do right now", Akshay cautioned Sam.

"I don't know. I can't work there anymore. It is so toxic. I drag myself every day to that place. This business will work out and I am very confident", Sam said with determination. There was silence for some time and all three left soon afterwards.

The next day, when Sam went to the office, his body language had changed. He was late as usual but had no fear of being bashed.

Meera looked at him and asked, "Late again? Pradeep was asking for you?"

"First of all, I am late or early, it is none of your business and are you Pradeep's secretary? If he was asking about me, he could call me", Sam said with a plain face and opened his laptop.

Everyone looked at each other wondering where this came from. Sam never spoke like this with anyone.

Sam was waiting for Pradeep to be free and was looking towards his cabin. Pradeep was in a meeting. The moment he got free, Sam got up from his chair and went straight to his cabin.

"Good morning sir! I need to speak to you", Sam said.

“If it is not urgent, can we talk later?”, Pradeep said looking at his mobile screen.

“It is very urgent”, Sam said looking at Pradeep.

“What is it?”Pradeep looked at Sam.

Sam sat in the chair and looked at Pradeep and said, “I am resigning”.

Pradeep thought he misheard. He asked to confirm, “What did you say?”.

“I am resigning from the job sir”, Sam said in a firmer voice.

“But, we had the conversation just Yesterday and I made it very clear, you don’t have to worry. So why this sudden decision?”, Pradeep seemed perplexed.

“Actually, I wanted to tell you this for a long time but could not find the right time. I had been thinking of starting my venture for some time now. I have some ideas and want to invest my time into it now”, Sam said.

“Oh is it? Entrepreneur!. Sounds cool. But I am wondering, you can not even handle basic work here and you want to start your venture”, Pradeep said in a sarcastic tone and burst into laughter.

Sam looked at Pradeep and cursed him in his mind. He smiled and said, “I will call you sir, if I need any help. I hope you will guide me like you always do”.

“Oh of course! But wait. Have you decided already?”, Pradeep asked.

"Yes sir and I shall put in my papers today and would like to serve a 30 days notice period as per the comp[any policy", Sam said in an affirmative voice.

"Give me some time. Let me discuss this with Rajeev. I will let you know tomorrow. And if you have already made up your mind, I shall not stop you, Wish you all the best. Let's speak tomorrow. I have to rush for a meeting", Pradeep said looking at his watch.

They both got up and Pradeep walked out of his cabin and Sam too. His face was exuberating with confidence and newfound energy.

Sam was however confident about his business venture but it was also an uncertain time for him. A lot was to be done.

Sam left office early that day and no one taunted him for that or said 'half-day'. He and Akshay had decided to meet in that cafe to discuss the next steps.

They had registered their business venture but the business plan was yet to be discussed. Who will do what, how will they contact clients, the database of clients, cold calling, setting up appointments, website, brochure, list of trainers and meeting them, these were just some of the many things they had to plan in the next few days.

Sam took most of the responsibilities as he had more time now, so he took the lead.

Sam started to compile the list of business schools in Delhi and nearby cities and started to call them to fix an appointment. Simultaneously, Ruchi had started to connect with soft skills trainers and compile a list of them. The website and brochure were Akshay's responsibility. Trio was all set to embark on their journey.

# CHAPTER 9

## *The Struggle*

**November 2008 onwards**

Sam was able to schedule some meetings. Their first meeting was in one week. And Sam's last working day was today.

Before leaving for the office, he prayed in the small temple at his home. He kept two pieces of paper there folded. He wrote 'job' in one and 'business' in one. After the prayer, he closed his eyes and picked up one of them. It was 'job' written inside. He did not agree with this decision. He wanted the blessings of the almighty god and it did not seem to go his way. So he closed his eyes again and picked up the paper again. It was 'job' written again. He was visibly confused and in disagreement with God's opinion on his career plans. This time, he kept his eyes open and deliberately picked up the paper written 'business' inside and said, "No one can change my mind now". He bowed his head in respect and left for the office.

Last working day in every company is always special and if it is someone's first job then it becomes even more special. Everyone wished him good luck for his future and a cake-cutting ceremony was held at the end of the day. Everyone said great words about him, his skills, his hard work and his knowledge. Sam was wondering about all this, "Where was all this appreciation all this while?", he asked himself.

The irony of working in the corporate world was unfolding in front of him.

In the evening, Sam met Akshay & Ruchi and they celebrated the official start of Sam's entrepreneurial journey. It was indeed an eventful day. A lot of things happened that day and it changed Sam's life forever.

The next three months were testing and also full of excitement. This is something Sam always dreamt of.

He was scheduling all the meetings and Ruchi would accompany him. Akshay would meet them after each meeting and discuss the outcome. Trio was not leaving any stone unturned to make their venture noticed and they were ready to give their everything to it.

***

It was Friday morning and Sam had to attend a meeting. Ruchi was not able to join as she was out of the station. Sam went alone and it did not go well.

He was travelling in the metro and called Ruchi to update her.

"Hey", Ruchi asked, "How did the meeting go?"

"Usual. You know the game now", Sam replied with a heavy voice.

"It's ok dude. Relax. One day, we shall make it", she tried to cheer him up.

"Yeah, I hope so. Where are you by the way? Are you back to Delhi?", Sam asked.

"Did Akshay not tell you? I am in Hyderabad. I moved here a week back. I have joined a financial firm as a Manager."

"What!!! What the fuck are you talking Ruchi? What about the business? What about all the dreams, all the plans we made together?", Sam was shocked. He was not able to decide if he should be happy for her and be sad for this stabbing in the back.

"Hey, relax. I can support you sitting here as well. My parents could have gotten me married elsewhere. So I took this job and moved here. Even Akshay is moving to Hyderabad next week. And we both can stay together. And moreover, a lot of businesses stay in Red before turning Green", Ruchi tried to explain.

Before Sam could say anything, the call got disconnected due to a weak network as Metro entered an underground tunnel.

This was a double whammy for Sam. He knew now, they had fooled him. They never quit their jobs nor did they stop him from quitting his job. Sam felt betrayed and was shattered now. The entire world seemed to have come crashing now. At this point, everything seemed to stand still.

Sam went back to his flat and cancelled the rest of the meetings for the day. He lay on the couch and closed his eyes. It has been four months now since he quit his job. His savings were dwindling. He had been only meeting clients but nothing fruitful had come so far. He realised he was too naive, amateur and impulsive. There was no mentor to guide him, no financial backup or any significant corporate experience.

Should he move on and start to look for a job and work on the business simultaneously or give a few more months to this business? Sam was in this dilemma.

Amidst all these thoughts, Sam dozed off.

He had a heavy head when he got up in the evening. The burden of his own expectations and dreams was pulling him down. Akshay & Ruchi were also not there to share it. His mind suddenly filled with rage. And then he started to cry and broke down in tears.

Sam did not want to be labelled as a loser and not lose hope. He decided to continue with his business and also try to find a part time job to support him financially. He knew, he will be fighting a lone battle and it is up to him to make a conscious choice. However, he did not write anything on a piece of paper this time. He had come too far for that choice now.

***

It was Saturday today and there were no meetings scheduled on that day. Sam got up with renewed desire and motivation. He wanted to change the name of the venture and develop a new website. That was his idea to rejuvenate. He knew this would keep him busy and give a new direction to his life.

For the next 6 months, Sam focused on changing and establishing the identity of the business venture with a new name. 'International Skill Consulting Group' and the new website he developed.

There were still no contracts and his savings were over long back. To support himself financially, he applied to many jobs but never got a call back from anywhere. He had been taking money from his brother and sister to pay for rent, food and other bills.

The month was November and Diwali was around the corner. It was the first time in his life, Sam was away from his family on Diwali. He was sitting in his room, penniless, empty stomach, with a broken heart and shattered dreams. The idea of business had backfired badly. And no one was ready to give him a job either.

The journey of an entrepreneur is never easy and Sam was experiencing it firsthand. What is the breaking point, No one knows. Depression and desperation can lead to unimaginable, unspeakable & inexplicable events. What matters is, how long can you hold on to the optimism and remain sound and sane.

Sam was feeling a bit low but definitely not defeated. He had this strange optimism, an ability to remain calm amidst the storm.

Sam was certain, one day he would taste success and this too shall pass. Nothing is permanent in this world, so does his life too. This is bound to change one day. Life can not be so harsh on him.

***

That year went by and still no luck for a job or any business deal. Sam could not borrow any more money from his brother and sister, so he started to sell his household things.

The year and date in the calendar had changed but the story was the same. Nothing had changed. Still no job and no business deal.

Sam had now applied to almost a thousand jobs but no one seemed to give him an interview opportunity.

But there was still something that kept Sam going. Basically, he did not have a choice but to keep going. So in the relentless pursuit of his dreams, he had accepted failures, his shortcomings, his naivety, and his impulse decisions and he learnt to look forward with full zeal and never lose hope.

***

It was 26th January today and a public holiday. Like every day, Sam got up and made tea for himself.

His mobile suddenly rang. Rohit NBA was the caller's name. Sam had been to NBA college for multiple meetings but nothing concrete had happened so far.

“Why is he calling today?”, Sam wondered and picked up the call.

“Hey Sam! Rohit here. How are you? Hope, I am not disturbing you early in the morning.”, Rohit said.

“No, not at all. Tell me”, Sam said.

“So can we start the training from next week if you are available?”, Rohit asked.

“What!! Training? Starting next week? Yes, yes. Sure, we can.”, Sam had excitement in his voice.

“Ok! Cool. Let me call you back in a while. I shall confirm the dates and logistics by evening. So finally we are doing training with you. Good luck and speak soon”, Rohit said and hung up.

Sam stood there for a while with his mobile in his hand. He kept staring at it. ‘So finally we are doing business with you’, these words were resonating in his mind on a loop. He thought he was dreaming. Tears rolled down from his eyes and then came an outburst. He cried his heart out that day.

The dream he had seen, the reality he had envisaged and the destiny he planned, finally he saw a glimpse of it. All the sufferings he had endured, all the gloomy feelings and all the futile efforts seemed to finally pay off today. Exactly one year since he quit his job and 18 months later he had started his venture with now-defunct business partners, there was a glimmer of hope. He did not know how big or significant this deal was or what were the challenges, but none of these mattered then. He was able to create something from scratch, and this experience transformed him as a person completely. There was a sense of satisfaction, a feeling of accomplishment, gratitude and more optimism.

# CHAPTER 10

## *Ship is Yet to Sail*

**November 2008 onwards**

But the excitement did not last long as the next call came from his father who informed him about the demise of his grandmother. She was very frail, unwell and over 100 years of age so the death was not very surprising but the timing of it was certainly painful.

Sam was worried about the clash of the training schedule with the travel plan to his hometown. Nonetheless, he had left for the town to attend his grandmother's funeral.

That evening when Sam was on the train, Rohit called him and confirmed the assignment details. The training was in 2 days and one day was already lost in the travel and the next day seemed to be washed away in funeral formalities.

Now the challenge was the execution. In the last year, Sam was focused only on getting appointments and getting a contract and now it was here, he did not know how to execute it.

He made a list of what he needs to deliver and the logistics he needs. And was shocked to find, except the contract, he did not have anything. His checklist included a trainer, training material, an assessment exam and most importantly, the money for all this and he had none of it.

But Sam was determined to not let go of this opportunity. He thought, if he could come this far from nowhere, then he should be able to handle this as well.

Sam decided to be the trainer for this assignment. He started to put together all the details of the training material and compile it. But where was the time to prepare the material and more important, money to get all this printed?

Whatever time Sam spent at home and on the trip back to Delhi, he put together a good draft of the training material from various sources. Now he moved to the next challenge of printing the training material.

He deliberated on this for a while and went to a nearby printer shop. He explained the situation to the shopkeeper and asked him if he can do it for free and if he can pay him when he gets the money after the training.

What was he expecting? At first, the shopkeeper was not even interested but Sam stood there. He told him how this is like a life and death situation and what this means to him. After a long persuasion, the shopkeeper agreed. He printed the entire course material.

The next day, Sam was there in the college in front of the students and delivering the training.

A dream was taking shape that day. And many dreams were taking birth. A journey that started 18 months back, had finally found its right path. The destination did not seem too far away.

Sam was standing there with a smile on his face and eyes shining as 'Founder Director of International Skill Consulting Group'. His eyes were brimming with millions of dreams and hope. His heart was full of pride. However, there was still a long way to go but the journey had begun already.

***

The next 6 months were like a fairytale for Sam. He received invitations for training from a lot of clients he had multiple meetings within the past year. Money was flowing and he was a busy man now. He was delivering a lot of training and travelling to many places to expand his business. He could see his dream taking shape slowly.

One fine day, he received an email from his MBA batchmate. He was starting a BPO unit (Business Process Outsourcing) and wanted Sam to be a part of it. BPO unit is a lucrative business if done right. But it requires an immense amount of business operations knowledge, business development skills and industry contacts. Sam had neither of them.

His batchmate Naresh who sent him the email claimed to be running two BPO units already in Bangalore and he needed partners & investment for the third one.

Sam travelled to Bangalore to meet Naresh. Naresh took him to his swanky office which floored Sam completely. He was certainly impressed and influenced by Naresh's success. They both had long meetings over the next three days and discussed various things from investments, business development and shareholding to partnership and expansion.

It all seemed like a natural progression to Sam. After Sam came back to Delhi, he could not take his mind off the BPO business. He decided to invest in Naresh's new BPO venture in Bangalore. Sam was aware of the risks as he was not aware of the functioning and ecosystem of the business process outsourcing. But he trusted Naresh and his instincts and invested everything he had earned from his training business.

# CHAPTER 11

## *The Fall*

**November 2008 onwards**

Sam was now heavily invested in the BPO and was making frequent trips to Bangalore every week. He did not have any business partner for his training business, hence he was not able to focus on it much. Sam did not bother either as he dreamt of big money from the BPO business as promised by Naresh.

***

It had been 6 months since Sam invested in the BPO business. He and Naresh also took funding from an overseas investor. Naresh was able to get some work from his contacts and the BPO operations were live. Over 100 associates were working in the BPO unit who were hired over the last 5 months.

Everything seemed just perfect except the profits. BPO unit was not making any profits and paying overhead costs including employee salary seemed an uphill task. Sam had exhausted all his savings already. Naresh was nowhere to be seen as he always kept busy in his other 2 BPO units.

One fine evening, when Sam was preparing an Excel sheet for the monthly expenses, he received a phone call from Naresh.

"Where the hell are you Man? I have been frantically trying to reach you for an hour", Naresh shouted from the other side.

"Relax! Maybe some network issue. What happened?", Sam tried to calm Naresh.

"We are doomed Sam. Everything is over", Naresh said in a frenzy.

'What do you mean by 'Everything is over'? Can you please relax and tell me what happened?", Sam stood up from his chair and asked while heading towards the balcony.

"Our client cheated on us. I had been sending emails and trying to reach his office for the last month, but that bugger never replied. Today from my sources, I got to know, he wrapped his office and ran away. He had taken money from many like us", Naresh told Sam.

Hearing this, Sam felt as if someone had taken away the ground below him and he was sinking. He felt as if his soul had left his body for a while. His face turned pale and he asked in an almost wailing tone, "What now Naresh?"

"I am sorry Sam. I pulled you into this knowing you had no idea about this business. I am at fault here", Naresh sounded apologetic.

"You did not understand me Naresh. I mean, what about the investment?", Sam asked.

"What about it?", Naresh asked.

"Have we lost all our money? Let me be specific here." Sam asked worryingly.

"Money! Dude, I am in deep debt. You remember John! That guy also invested in our BPO unit. He has been behind my life for the last 5 months. I have no idea how I would tell him. He will shoot me", Naresh said and hung up.

Sam tried to call Naresh, but his phone was switched off. He tried for the next one hour but to no avail.

Sam was back to ground zero where he started almost two and a half years back. He had lost everything he had earned and now was also in deep debt. He had no leads for any training as he had not focused on it for the last 6 months and whosoever approached him for training, he turned them down saying he was busy.

Sam travelled to Bangalore the next day. The office was empty and no one could be found there. He called a few of the staff members and employees but most of the numbers were switched off or busy. He went to Naresh's house and got to know, he moved out a week back.

Sam was now in languishing pain. He went back to the office, sat in the office and started to cry. He felt as if his heart would explode.

Did Naresh cheat on him? Is he so naive that he trusts people easily and gives away everything like an idiot? Will he ever be successful? He kept asking & repeating these questions to himself.

For a moment he thought of filing a criminal case against Naresh. But he also knew he does not have neither time, money or energy left.

He took the flight back to Delhi the same night. Sam knew he had to collect the pieces of his life again and start life from scratch.

# CHAPTER 12

## The Comeback

**November 2008 onwards**

Sam had no money left with him, and with no savings and no business leads, he had come back to the same place he had started over two and half years back, like a full circle. He started to connect with his old clients and resume the training business. But he had been out for good 6 months and a lot of them had moved on to other training providers. Sam knew it would happen but there was no option but to keep trying.

Meanwhile, he also started to apply for jobs like he did a year ago but some things do not change in life irrespective of all the life changes.

Sam kept applying for jobs for the next 3 months but did not get a single interview invitation. He had again started to sell his household things to stay alive, pay bills and manage food. He could not gather the courage to inform his sister, brother or parents as they would have certainly accused him of being naive, greedy and a complete idiot.

"How did he not learn his lessons the first time when his earlier business partners left him?", this would definitely be a common theme of all the discussions with everyone who knew him. Hence, Sam decided to keep this failure a secret until he comes out of it one day.

***

After 4 month's struggle, Sam was finally able to get a training assignment.

Nothing had changed indeed. All struggles, all challenges, everything was the same even after almost 3 years since he started the venture.

But this time, Sam was determined to not let go. He worked extremely hard on that assignment. He had realised his true strengths and wanted to focus completely on the training business now.

For the next year, Sam spent his entire energy expanding the footprints of his business across India. He travelled to many cities and connected with business schools. His sole focus was to establish himself as a serious player in the soft skills industry for business schools.

Sam's hard word indeed paid off well too. He would do free awareness sessions for clients and due to his great oratory skills, he could get a lot of clients.

Life seemed to be back on track but every business has its own uncertainties. Money had started to flow in but Sam was being extra cautious this time. There were times when clients' money got late by many weeks and he had to survive on savings. This was a fact that was not giving him a lot of confidence to be able to make it big.

External investment was out of the question as they say, 'once bitten, twice shy', Sam indeed was now averse to any external funding or having an extra pair of hands in the business as a partner.

Sam was not against going back to the corporate world and pursuing a full-time career but in the last 4 years, despite his best efforts and after applying for over 2000 jobs, he had no hopes left.

It was September month of 2013. He was sitting on the couch and looking at his bank statement and taking stock of his savings. There were no training assignments in sight for another 3 months and savings were not enough to survive that long. He took a deep breath and lay on the couch. He closed his eyes and started to wonder about the outcome of the last 4 years.

His learning was immense. These 4 years taught him some invaluable life lessons something any B-school in the world could never teach. Life was his best teacher in those years. The impeccable maturity and self-belief, steel-like mental stability and strength and staying optimistic amidst the worst, were some of the very best life learnings he could gain in the last few years. He has become a version of himself which could have taken another 10-15 years under normal circumstances but he went through the test of fire not once but 4 long years.

Yet there was no financial success. He had seen it all. The shattered dreams, hungry stomach, empty pockets and a broken heart. Success had still eluded him. He may have been a role model for many for his determination and entrepreneurial skills but this would not pay his bills he knew. He had been featured in many newspapers for conducting workshops and spreading awareness of game-changing employability skills and even got him an interview in a leading magazine, but, still this did not convert into a profitable business or even a job for that matter.

Something was still missing. His due from life was still pending. Sam was the ideal partner every girl would have loved to have in her life, a business associate an entrepreneur would want and an employee who would be an asset. Alas, he had a lot to offer but there were no takers.

His phone suddenly rang and his thoughts came to a halt. He picked up and a female voice said in a soft tone, "Am I talking to Samrat Sharma?"

"Yes", Sam answered.

"Hi Samrat. I am Shashi calling from Azamon. And this is regarding a job opening for our Hyderabad office. Would you be interested?", Shashi introduced herself.

Hell yes, Sam wanted to say but he kept his excitement to himself and answered, "Yes! Sure. What is the job profile?".

Shashi explained the role to Sam and it sounded interesting to him. He thought he was made for this role. He also got to know, Azamon was looking for a suitable candidate for this role for over 1.5 years but no one could crack the role yet.

Sam said yes and Shashi hung up saying she will schedule further rounds.

Sam was in disbelief. He thought he was dreaming or hallucinating. Azamon was the biggest e-commerce firm in the world and one of the best companies to work for. People would kill to work in this company and he got a call for a role which was most sought after and none could qualify for over 1.5 years.

And for the first time in the last 4 and half years, Sam thought of quitting his business and shutting it down forever. Easier thought than done. This was Sam's child in the truest sense. He had created it from scratch, from an idea, withstood all challenges, went down many times and got up again, learnt the most valuable lessons of his life and now he was thinking to quit, when there could be a turning point. But what was the turning point?

Turning down to appear for the job interview for the most valuable company on earth and continuing the business or closing the business and looking for jobs, could have been the real turning point for a disaster for sure.

Deep down in his heart, Sam had already believed this job belonged to him. There was a strange belief and confidence.

And then Sam did what was unimaginable until a day back. He called Packers and Movers and planned to shift all his belongings to his home town in Bareilly. Sam's mind had already believed the job in Azamon was his and he wanted no baggage. He had decided to close his business and focus on job interviews.

Upon reaching Bareilly, Sam's parents were in disbelief after Sam told them everything. They did not want to discourage him but they also knew that's not how things work in real life. However, for Sam, things never did work in a typical manner anyways in the real world.

# CHAPTER 13

## *The Second Inning*

**November 2013**

Sam indeed got the job in Azamon despite all odds and shifted to Hyderabad to start a new chapter in his life. One day before his joining day, Sam was sitting in his hotel room. His second inning of life was about to begin the very next day.

Sitting in that room, looking outside the window, Sam had only one thought and he said to himself, "You have finally arrived Sam. You did it. This was the destination you had been waiting for so long. Your penance for the last 4 years has paid off. Your life begins here". There were no tears in his eyes but a big warrior-like smile, and indeed it was. A war had been won.

***

The next few years were like a fairy-tale story in Sam's life. He did really well in his job. Infact, his personal life also seemed to get back on track.

Sam fell in love with his old friend who was an entrepreneur like him and they got married within 8 months of Sam starting his new life. It was indeed like a fairy-tale for Sam who had seen the worst in his life and now seeing the greener patches.

Life continued for him. He changed jobs. His wife also expanded her business, and she was doing well. It all looked picture perfect but as they say, "This too shall pass" and it indeed did.

Sam's mother was diagnosed with lung cancer, and she was at the last stage. This news came like a lightning strike. His life suddenly turned upside down. He brought his mother to Hyderabad for treatment, but she could not withstand the pain and passed away in six months.

The toil, stress and the changed dynamics impacted his relationship with his wife, who was a frequent traveller and very busy in her business, and found another shoulder to share her life.

She asked for a divorce. Sam was in a state of shock already and the demise of her mother was too much to digest, and this divorce sounded like adding salt to the injury.

Things were not smooth between him and his life, but divorce was the last thing he could have imagined. His wife felt Sam was not able to support her financially, emotionally and physically. Yes, there was no sex life. The old flame had vanished, and she was quick to move on with her business partner.

Sam did not want the divorce, but she was adamant. She threatened him with dire consequences if he does not agree to the divorce. Sam had to give in to the pressure.

His wife took away the house they purchased together, all the things they bought to decorate it with and asked for a huge alimony. He had to take a huge loan to pay her the sum she asked for and was left only with his books which he could have never given away. He considered his books his soul.

Sam was thrown out of his own house. Once more, life had made a mockery of him, yet there he was, not complaining, standing tall and strong in the face of his adversaries.

Sam got divorced within six months. But by now Sam knew how to rise from the ashes. He again had to start from scratch and collect the pieces of his life together.

Sam had to prepare for the third inning of his life now.

# CHAPTER 14

## *Badrinath*

**16th May 2018**

Upon reaching home, Sam could not sleep. Whatever drinks he had, made no impact. He was in a flashback. But more than that, it was a storm of thoughts. He was hanging between the past and present. What he had become after his divorce, a mean, cold heart, materialistic asshole. Something similar Preeti told him Yesterday. She was not wrong either, but Sam had no qualms about it.

"Why should I care about anyone or what people think about me? Where was everyone, when I was going through the lowest point of my life? It's my life and no one, absolutely no one, has any right to tell me how to live my life. They can go fuck themselves. Maybe Preeti needs more sex from her husband, huh. Her hormones seem to be oozing out. Bloody bitch", Sam murmured in a sarcastic tone while making a drink for himself.

"Let me see who is this Sai Kiran. What is this all about?", Sam said while opening his laptop. He searched for 'Sai Kiran, author of a book titled unknown' on google. The first few results were enough to quench his thirst for this query. Theywere providing references to some websites where this book was available. It also showed some video results and one of them was the same documentary Sam watched this afternoon.

He clicked on one of the search results which led him to a blog, saiwritings.blogspot.com.

Sam started browsing through the blog. He was now convinced; it was the same Sai he saw in that documentary. There were many posts. "This Sai guy seems to be spiritual. Most of his posts are around such topics", Sam said, sipping his whiskey glass. "Is there anything he wrote about his trip?", Sai wondered while scrolling down the blog.

"Trip to Badrinath. I see one post, cool. A new beginning, what's that?"Sam opened the blog post titled 'A new beginning', written on 17th March 2002.

As Sam started reading that post, his eyes and mouth opened wide.

It was the same Sai whose documentary Sam watched this afternoon. Sai had mentioned his experience after his meeting with that strange man in the Badrinath. His sleep had been disturbed completely, and he had been getting some visions and nightmares both. In his dreams, he found himself in the Badrinath, wandering aimlessly in the wilderness. Sai was clueless about what was happening to him. There was a constant void he had been feeling and this feeling of disconnecting from everyone and everything had grown.

The words of that mystic were ringing in his head constantly, you were seeking me, so you found me. After going through this ordeal for 6 months, Sai decided to visit Badrinath again, hoping to see that mystic again.

Sai left his home on 3rd April 2002. The next post was titled "The Seeker" and that's it. There was no content in it. Nothing was written afterwards. This was the last post from Sai on his blog.

Sam was not a spiritual guy nor a religious one. But he found this instance very adventurous and interesting. He has slogged his ass for 5 months straight on this new project. It got over last week, and he had planned for a short break before he got back to the grind again.

"Looks like I found my next adventure. If I tell Rohit, I am going to Badrinath, he might get a mini heart attack", Sam told himself and started laughing.

It was 1 AM, but sleep was miles away from Sam's eyes. His whiskey glass was empty. He poured some more whiskey into his glass and headed to his balcony. The moment Sam stepped into the balcony, he first looked around to see if that old man was nearby. He tried to see through the blanket of darkness in the empty land, but there was no one. He sighed with a relief, and had a big sip from his whiskey glass.

Sam stood there, lost in his thoughts. It was hot and humid outside. The memories of the past came back again to haunt him. It has been 3 years, but his mind never let him forget the day destiny made him taste the ground again, after his 3 years old marriage. He had tried hard to absorb himself in the work, travel, parties and all sorts of distractions, but he could never take his mind off all the sufferings, insults and losses, financially, emotionally and mentally, he had to endure.

"I just want to run away from all this. Somewhere, far off, in the mountains, just be there in the wilderness, do nothing. No stress about job, money, marriage, career, fights. I just want to live my own life;

Sam was talking in his mind. "Just wrap some leaves around your waist and you are good to go. And if you feel hungry, eat those leaves too. What a life Sam", He started laughing at this thought.

"But, what about Ayesha? She likes you a lot. And you have to finish Game of Thrones and Money Heist also", Sam was talking to himself. He was in a hilarious dilemma.

"Ayesha will still be there, and all the series can also wait. I am going to Badrinath, no matter what", Sam said to himself in an affirmative tone, came back to his room and went to sleep

# CHAPTER 15

## The Company

**17th May 2018**

"I got my first real six string, bought it at the five and dime, played it till my fingers bled, it was the summer of '69". Brain Adam's famous song was the ringtone on Sam's phone and it rang at 9 AM in the morning.

"Hello", Sam answered the phone half awake.

"Who else, darling Rohit", Rohit said laughing. "I called to check on you if you were feeling alright. You left suddenly last night".

"I am fine buddy. Just wanted some ME time. Sorry for last night".

"Chill dude. Just kidding. What's your plan for today?", Rohit asked.

"I will just rest today. No plans but will stay at home". Sam replied.

"Cool. Take care and call me if you change your mind", Rohit said and hung up.

Sam was still in his bed. His head was heavy. He was still in last night's thoughts. He got up from his bed and went straight to the kitchen. He made coffee for himself and came to his balcony and leaned on the railings facing towards the empty land.

"So, this is where it all began", Sam said to himself sipping his coffee. He was wondering about the events of the last 2 days. A lot happened in the last 2 days. He was not able to decide if it was real or his imagination. Was it really happening?

"Do you seriously want to visit Badrinath? Have you lost your mind?", Sam was again talking to himself.

"You wanted to go to Goa and now you are planning to go to Badrinath. Your friends will disown you for sure", Sam started smiling on this hilarious tussle inside his mind.

"So Badrinath it is. But wait, where will I go in Badrinath? What will I do there? I just saw a strange man in my dreams, saw his picture in a god-forbidden novel, watched a crap documentary and now I have decided to travel Badrinath. Where is all this coming from and where does it lead?". This tussle was slowly becoming a tug-of-war between stupidity and adventure.

"I am not going to visit any temple there. I will do some hiking and stay in a good resort. That's it. It's a beautiful place after all and heat is killing us anyways right now. It will be a good break", Sam tried to convince himself and he seemed convinced too when he started checking the route to Badrinath and searched 'how to travel to Badrinath from Delhi' on google?

***

Reaching Badrinath from Delhi is not easy. One needs to take a flight from Delhi to Dehradun Airport and then board a cab. This entire trip can easily take 12-15 hours if the road and weather conditions are good, else one can get stuck for hours and in the worst case, days, like Sai & his friends from the documentary.

For Sam, it was more of an adventure trip and he was very excited. He had travelled to many places in the world for work and leisure, but this was different. First time in his life, he had an unknown motive and urge to find a context. This was very thrilling for him and he always liked challenges. So Sam decided to drive to Badrinath. Though he was unaware of the challenges ahead, long drives always enthralled him and a road less travelled, this trip to Badrinath, was going to change his life forever.

***

Next week, Sam informed his manager about his upcoming travel plans and took a complete week off from 4-11 June. He had not informed anyone about his travel, not even his parents and Rohit as well. He only said it's a secret when Rohit asked him, where is he travelling to and why such a sudden plan?

Rohit was more than certain; Sam was going to meet a girl in some city. He could have never imagined Badrinath and Sam going there was beyond his belief system.

Sam knew it and he did not want too many questions or any second thoughts. So, he did not reveal his plans. He just mentioned a hill resort to escape from Delhi's scorching heat.

It won't be a big surprise for readers to know that Sam decided to drive till Badrinath. After all, this was not a pilgrim trip for him. Who cares if it was a pilgrim, it had to be a lifetime experience.

Unlike any other traveller, Sam had just decided to have a backpack and a small bag of his clothes and other essentials for the trip. He was all set to embark upon the most important, soul-fulfilling, gut-wrenching and life changing journey.

# CHAPTER 16

## The Journey

**4th June 2018**

*'the journey of a thousand miles,*
*always begins with a single step'*

In order to discover oneself, one needs to leave one's most prized possessions. And this is exactly Sam was about to do, unaware though.

Sam started his journey on 4th June 2018 from Delhi at 4 AM. It was a 500 KM route, out of which almost 250 km drive was in plains till Haridwar, another significant Hindu pilgrimage.

After Haridwar, driving gets tricky as it is a mountainous region. From Haridwar, one drives to Rishikesh and then it gets further difficult as that area is landslide-prone.

Sam was travelling in June and the monsoon was around the corner. There were high chances of heavy rains, flash floods and landslides. All these conditions led to the disaster in Kedarnath, another nearby sacred Hindu pilgrimage in June 2013. Cloud bursts, heavy rains and multiple landslides had ravaged the entire region and thousands died and many are still missing. Nature showed no mercy and wreaked havoc.

Sam was aware of this fact as he did his research. It was indeed a daunting task to drive from Delhi to Badrinath and come back unscathed. But spirits were high and all this pumped-up Sam's adrenaline high.

Sam wanted to reach Haridwar by 10 am. Breakfast amidst nature was on his mind. And in fact, when one drives to this region and nears Haridwar, they cannot miss the eternal natural beauty.  It is refreshing and divine in all essence.

As he wanted to avoid the Delhi traffic, he started early. And by 6:30 PM, he had reached Muzaffarnagar city in Uttar Pradesh state.

In summer, the Sun god rises early but the heat is not scorching until 12 PM. It was a beautiful morning and the sun was still rising.

Sam was on the outskirts of the town, a state highway. It had been long since Sam witnessed sunrise. He was never a morning person and it was too early for him to be out of his bed let alone the city. But it is not the destination but the journey that enthrals everyone. And, same was the case with Sam. Empty roads can make any trip exciting.

Sam was out of town and coffee was his morning routine. He had been drowsy for some time now. He started to look for a coffee stall on the way and soon he found a tea stall roadside. He parked his car on the side and got out of the car.

His lungs filled with humid air and the smell of mustard plants. He looked around. That entire place was yellow and brimming with mustard plants. It was a beautiful sight and he then realised; It has been long since he experienced nature in its true form. He remembered, during his childhood, whenever he visited his maternal grandmother, he would play in mustard fields all day. That little memory brought a smile to his face. He was not drowsy anymore.

“Do you have coffee?”, Sam asked the tea vendor.

“No sir, only tea," the vendor replied.

“Hhmm, okay. One tea in a big cup, if you have”, Sam ordered.

“It will be 20 rupees sir”, the vendor told him the rate before confirming the order.

“Yeah, yeah, go ahead”, Sam said.

“Ok, give me 5 minutes. I shall make fresh tea for you. Where are you travelling sir to?”, the tea vendor asked.

“Badrinath”, Sam replied looking at his mobile screen.

“Oh, that is very far but it is a very beautiful place, sir. I have never visited but I want to visit Shiv Baba one day. Can I request something sir?", the tea vendor urged Sam.

Sam looked at the vendor with amusement and said "Yeah, tell me".

"If I give you money, could you please offer it to Lord Shiv on my behalf? And you don't have to pay for this tea sir, it is on me now.", the tea vendor requested with a smile.

"Uumm, I am actually not going to Badrinath temple. I am going to a resort there", Sam clarified.

"What?"The tea vendor was surprised and had his mouth wide open.

"Resort in Badrinath! You will go to Badrinath to stay in a resort and not visit Shiv baba. What are you saying sir? How is this possible? I have been trying my whole life to go there and still not able to go and here you are, going to Badrinath to stay in a resort. What kind of people are there in this world?"The tea vendor was visibly annoyed.

"And please, this tea is not for free. Please pay 20 rupees", the tea vendor handed over the tea to Sam and asked in an authoritative and irritated tone.

All this while Sam was clueless. He did not know his response would evoke so many emotions in that tea vendor. He chose to stay silent. He paid him 20 rupees and walked to the other side of the road. He also realised that he is not supposed to tell people about this trip.

"Good, I did not talk about this trip to anyone. I knew this was coming. Anyways, calm down Sam. Enjoy your tea. It is a beautiful morning, do not ruin your mood. You already knew it.", he murmured.

He finished his tea and resumed his journey from Muzaffarnagar to Haridwar, another 100 km from there.

***

Sam took another 2.5 hours to reach Haridwar, an ancient city and important Hindu pilgrimage site in North India's Uttarakhand state, where the River Ganges exits the Himalayan foothills. The largest of several sacred ghats (bathing steps), Har Ki Pauri hosts a nightly Ganga Aarti (river-worshipping ceremony) in which tiny flickering lamps are floated off the steps. Worshipers fill the city during major festivals including the annual Kanwar Mela.

This city has majestic vibes. It is a perfect amalgamation of history, culture, and ethnicity. It has witnessed many civilizations, been ravaged many times and still stood its ground. And Sam was finally here, in the city of Lord Shiva, still 300 km away from his destination.

It was 9:15 AM. Sam wanted to avoid the traffic inside the city, so he kept himself away from city roads and took an aerial route. He was hungry too, so he was looking for a food joint on the way. He soon found one, Vaishno Shudh Desi Dhaba.

Such Vaishno dhabas were very common in Haridwar and one can find numerous dhabas with the same name at almost every 100 metres. Sam parked his car there and went inside.

It was a typical roadside food joint. There were many tourists inside and to Sam's surprise there were many foreigners as well. Haridwar is a very big and significant Hindu pilgrimage, and it is visited by millions of devotees and spiritual seekers across the globe every year.

Sam wanted to eat something quickly and resume his journey from there at the earliest. He ordered Aloo paratha and a cup of tea. And this time, no one asked him about his travel plans. He looked around for a place to sit and found an empty two-seater table in a corner. The moment he sat there, a middle-aged man came from behind and asked him if the chair across him was occupied. Sai nodded his head and said no one is sitting here.

Sam was hoping only for one thing and that was a question on his travel plans and he started getting edgy while that man sipped his tea In Front of him. "Hey, I am Sai ", that guy introduced himself.

Sam almost jumped out of his chair and tea in his mouth almost came out like a volcano erupting from one side. “Sai Kiran?”, Sam asked hesitatingly and also with a curiosity in his voice.

“No, Sai Krishna. Were you expecting to meet someone here?”, Sai asked.

“No nothing. No one.”, Sam replied hastily.

“Actually, Sai is a very common name in India”, Sai said.

“Yeah, yeah. Ok, I need to leave, still, a lot of distance to cover”, Sam said and got up.

“Oh, where are you travelling to?”Sai asked.

Sam’s face was cold and red with irritation. “I am just a tourist here, came to meet some friends, that’s it”, Sam said and left. He paid the bill and looked at that table from the corner of his left eye. Sai was still sitting there, looking outside the window and sipping his tea.

Sai looked at Sam and Sam turned his head to his right as if he did not see anything. He quickly left that food joint and resumed his journey from there. The next stop was Rishikesh.

Rishikesh is a city in India’s northern state of Uttarakhand, in the Himalayan foothills beside the Ganges River. The river is considered holy, and the city is renowned as a centre for studying yoga and meditation. Temples and ashrams (centres for spiritual studies) line the eastern bank around Swarg Ashram, a traffic-free, alcohol-free and vegetarian enclave upstream from Rishikesh town.

Rishikesh is close to 30 Km from Haridwar and takes only almost an hour to reach. Sam had no plans to take another break in Rishikesh, but he wanted to visit a café, named Musafir cafe en route.

Long back, when he was in college, he had been there. He thought to cherish his college memories of visiting Musafir cafe and resume his journey from there.

***

Musafir cafe in Rishikesh, is a lively place, bustling with tourists all the time. Like Haridwar, Rishikesh is also visited by tourists and devotees from all across the world.

Everyone who visits this town has something to look forward to. Some seek nirvana here; some seek adventure while some are here just to escape from the summer heat of towns like Delhi. Sam was there for none of those reasons. For him, it was a simple time travel in his past.

Sam last visited this cafe in 2004 during his college days and it had been 14 years since then, but nothing had changed there. Roads and other infrastructure were better but the city, its buildings and culture had remained absolutely the same.

Sam parked his car outside. He remembered last time when he visited, there used to be a lawn outside the cafe which was not converted into a parking lot. Of course, the musafir cafe had grown in size and popularity.

He went inside, stood in a corner for a while, looked around, trying to familiarise himself with his surroundings and remembering the old days.

The furniture seemed new, the paint on the wall was recently done. He took a deep breath and found an empty seat near the main door and sat there.

It was a cold morning in Rishikesh. The temperature was hovering around 8 degrees Celsius. Sam ordered a coffee for himself.

Before he could taste that warm coffee, a heavy voice brought him back from his memories.

"Excuse me, is that seat occupied?". A tall, lean and young guy with long hair till shoulders, who seemed to be in his early twenties was standing in front of him.

"No, it is not", Sam replied.

"Thank you. Would you mind if I sit here?", that young guy asked.

"It's alright", Sam replied without looking at him and took a sip from his coffee. This time, Sam thought to strike up a conversation with that guy, not because he was bored but because he wanted to avoid getting asked questions about his travel plans.

"So, are you here for fun like river rafting or something", Sam asked.

"Not exactly", that guy replied, "Oh, and my name is Anand".

"I am Sam. So, what are you doing here, Anand?", Sam asked.

"I work in a Hydropower project in Lambagad. It is near Badrinath dham, if you have heard of this place". Anand replied.

"Not Lambagad, but Badrinath I have heard of. I am travelling to that place only. And, before you ask anything else, let me clarify, I am not visiting Badrinath for lord shiva. I am neither spiritual nor religious. I was just bored at work and it is too hot right now in Delhi. So, I am just travelling to take a small break from all the hassles.

"Hahahahahah", Anand laughed hard. "Dude, it's alright. I am not judging you, So, relax. There are a lot of good places to see around Badrinath. In fact, on your way to Badrinath, you will come across many beautiful sights, waterfalls and nature at its best. So, did you drive here or took a bus?", Anand asked.

"I drove here", Sam replied.

"Be careful on the way. This is not the best time to travel as it starts raining and landslides are very common in that region. And if you get stuck in one of them, you will curse the day you planned to travel to Badrinath", Anand cautioned Sam.

"So, if you just want to take a break and enjoy the wintery weather, you are already at the best place. Rishikesh is no less than Badrinath. It is very tricky to drive and can get very dangerous as well. I shall suggest, you spend some time here and go back to Delhi after a few days".

Sam was listening patiently to Anand. He was indeed making sense, but his heart was thinking otherwise. It was not just a break, an escape from the summer heat but something else that drove him here. He did not know what it was, but he wanted to give it a try.

"You are right, but I would still like to give it a try. It will be fun, and I shall be alright. But I appreciate your concern and your advice", Sam said to Anand smiling and got up.

"So, for how long are you here? Are you here on vacation?", Sam asked Anand.

"I came here to meet some friends and I shall go back now", Anand replied.

"And how will you go back?", Sam asked.

"I shall take a taxi. It's the best way to travel here." Anand said smiling.

"If you are comfortable and don't mind, I can drop you at your power station. You had mentioned it is on the way if I heard right", Sam suggested to Anand.

"It is on the way but it will not be easy for you to drive there. And god forbid, if there is any landslide on the way, we both shall get stuck and I won't be able to leave you like this on the way then", Anand said hesitatingly.

"Dude, relax. Don't be so scared. I know what you mean but you can get stuck in a taxi also. And if it happens also, don't worry, I won't blame you. And, by the way, I am not that bad driver", Sam winked and smiled at Anand.

Both laughed hard. They both paid their bills and walked out of the Musafir cafe. Since the time Sam started the trip early in the morning, he felt joyful knowing he has the company of someone who knows the region and is not judging him for travelling to Badrinath without visiting Lord Shiva.

***

# CHAPTER 17

## *The Warning*

**4th June 2018**

Rishikesh to Badrinath is almost 300 km but the road is very treacherous. And as cautioned by Anand, it can get extremely dangerous if it rains or snow falls and worse, if the landslides. However, the duo of Anand and Sam was oblivious to any dangers and were enjoying the natural beauty of Rishikesh as they were driving through.

"So, you come here very often?", Sam asked Anand.

"I come here on weekends if I am free. I meet some people, buy some groceries, medicines and anything else I need. We don't get these things where I stay", Anand replied.

"I can understand. How is life where you come from? I am sure, it is definitely not like what I get to live in Delhi", Sam asked with curiosity.

Anand laughed out loud and said, "Of course, what you do in Delhi is not life; it is rather a grind, a run-of-a-mill job. It looks like you guys are just spending days and one day you will die without even knowing why you were here. In fact I feel, you live the same day for most of your lives without even realising. So, living a life with purpose and spending days being busy paying bills are two different things, my friend", Anand replied with a serious tone.

"What do you mean by spending days and dying without knowing why I was here?", Sam asked in a cynical tone.

"Ok, let me ask you. What do you think your purpose in this life is?", Anand asked.

"Honestly speaking, to earn a lot of money, be able to lead a satisfying life, become successful in my career, be able to fulfil all my dreams and yes, enjoy every moment, that's what I think is the purpose of my life and I guess the purpose of everyone in this world", Sam replied with a shine is his eyes.

"Makes sense if you think all this is real", Anand said looking out of the window.

"Real? What is not real. I am 100% real, and this Adidas jacket is more than real. Don't tell me you are a ghost", Sam started laughing and looked at Anand mockingly.

"What if I tell you, everything that you think is an illusion and you are living in a dream?", Anand asked

Sam, “And your experience of reality is the biggest lie you have ever known”

There was a big truck in front of them that suddenly applied a brake and stopped. Fortunately, Sam was driving slowly so nothing happened.

“Do you think that a truck suddenly applying brakes in front of us is an illusion? Dude, we could have become an illusion in a few seconds had I not applied the brakes now. I wish my boss was an illusion, but right now my salary looks like an illusion to me. When it comes, when it goes, no idea”, Sam sighed and uttered some expletives for the truck driver ahead.

“Can you please not talk in riddles? Ok, you tell me. What is your purpose here? You work in a power plant, you told me. isn’t it?”, Sam asked Anand, navigating his way around that truck.

Anand did not reply immediately. He was looking outside the window and kept looking for the next few seconds. “Excuse me, Sir! I am talking to you.” Sam shook Anand’s arm and spoke.

“Oh, I am sorry”, Anand apologised and replied, “I was thinking something, so missed your question”.

“Thank god, you are not the driver”, Sam said sarcastically.

“So, you asked what my purpose is. I think mine and your purpose are the same. Right now, you need to reach Badrinath, and I have to get down mid-way, so our purpose is to reach our destination. However, our physical destination may be different but our spiritual destination is the same", Anand said in a deep voice.

"Hello, hello. English please", Sam said laughing. "What is this spiritual & physical destination? You know what, had you met my friend Rohit, he would have gone crazy listening to all this and would have probably jumped out off this cliff", Sam said and started laughing.

"I know, it all sounds crazy and meaningless until you experience it on your own. My experience will sound like a crazy story which you will not believe at all. But it is not the question of belief, but personal experience", Anand said while looking out of the window.

"Why don't you explain all this to me like a layman? But I am interested to understand this illusion and the real stuff you were talking about", Sam asked.

"Let me ask you something. How do you define something as real?", Anand asked.

"I can touch, feel, smell, see and hear it like I can see you, hear you. Dude, please don't turn out to be a ghost", Sam winked and started laughing.

Anand also smiled and said, "You are correct. What you mentioned, are all our senses and we use them to construct our reality. Imagine a blind, deaf and dumb man who does not have hands either. How will this person construct reality? If I also add the loss of smell and taste, then this person will look at the world differently. There will be no difference between beautiful and ugly, bitter & sweet, big or small, foul smell or good odour, none of these will exist, as this person will not be able to use his sensory organs to perceive the world as we do".

"Hold on. But this person is disabled. So, it is natural for him to perceive the world differently", Sam interrupted Anand and showed his curiosity.

"You are right. What I was trying to say, is how the lack of senses will lead to a different perception of reality", Anand clarified.

"I get that. What is the point here? I have all my senses working fine. And why would I or for that matter, anyone would like to lose his senses? What will I achieve by losing them?", Sam was now getting indulged in the discussion.

"Now we are talking", Anand said with a shine in his eyes. "Since we took birth, we have been conditioned to see the world in a certain way and that behaviour led us to a certain reality. The only purpose we think is to get a high-paying job, bigger house, more money, new clothes and car and what not. And there is no end to it, the more we get, the more we want. Our mind is filled with images and those images are our reality".

"So, what's wrong with it?", Sam asked, "Everyone is doing it. Everyone wants to lead a good life and give a better life to his or her loved ones. We get an education so that we can build a good life for ourselves and retire with good money, live healthily and die peacefully. Look around you dude. There is so much competition outside. In my office, to get a 10% hike in salary, you need to literally work your ass off and promotion is a really big deal. I don't know what happens in your world but in my world, this is a definite reality and not an illusion. The only illusion in my world is a peaceful day without any firefighting issues", Sam sounded irritated.

"And? Do you enjoy all this? This feeling of working like an Ass, having so much stress and all that, do you really want all that?", Anand asked.

"What options do we have? Isn't this what everyone is doing? Isn't this something everyone wants to do? Everyone wants luxury and comfort in life and to get this, you need to work hard. I am not able to understand, why are you against it?", Sam was amused.

"You got me wrong here. There is nothing wrong with living a luxurious life or wanting comfort. My point is about attachment. The more you get attached to anything, any object, any feeling, the more you suffer. That was the whole point that you missed", Anand explained.

"Attachment as in?", Sam asked with curiosity.

"So, whatever you just mentioned, you like to do all of it and repeat it and expect a result that gives you some satisfaction or a high or some sense of gratification. Correct?", Anand asked.

"It isn't obvious if you do something, you will expect something in return. Why will I work if I don't get paid", Sam replied sarcastically.

"Imagine a situation. You have been working very hard on a project and putting in your best efforts. But you were not expecting anything in return, I mean, an appreciation, a monetary reward or a promotion", Anand put a situation In Front of Sam to explain his point.

Sam burst with laughter, "Dude, you must be out of your mind. People these days don't even blink an eye if they don't know what's in it for them. Every fucking guy I know, is working for something and definitely expects something in return. Why should we not expect it if we work so hard. My boss gives me peanuts in annual appraisal anyways and if he gets to know I am not expecting anything, he will give me real peanuts in appraisal", Sam said and started hysterically.

"I am now getting confused, dude. You started with real and illusion stuff. Then you talked about purpose and now you are talking about attachment. What exactly is your point? Do you even know what you have been talking.", Sam asked Anand in a mocking tone.

Anand laughed hard and his face suddenly became serious. He said, "We are all in a deep sleep Sam. All this you feel, see and experience is all an illusion. Your construct of reality is standing on an illusion. It is all a big dream. I am half awake and you are still in deep sleep, so you are not able to believe or realise anything I said. But the point is, will you ever be able to wake up and find your true destiny? What does it mean to wake up? What happens when we realise it was all a dream? Can we go back to this dream again or do we ever want to go back? I do not have all the answers, but I know one thing for a fact, the bliss and pleasure when you wake up is so strong, you will never like to sleep again. And at the moment, every word I said will resonate in your mind"

He continued, "All the sufferings, all the sorrows, all the grief will stay until you know who you are and what is your purpose. And let me tell you something, you did not come here because it was very hot in Delhi or you were bored. You came here because you were seeking something and more than you, something was seeking you".

Anand turned his head towards the left window. Sam suddenly applied for a break. He could not decide what prompted him to do so, the motorbike coming in the wrong direction or the last statement made by Anand. His hands just froze at the steering wheel. There was a dead silence in the car. No one was looking at each other. Sam's face was cold and deadly serious.

Hundreds of thoughts were doing salsa in his head. 'This guy is crazy', 'Maybe he hates his job or lost his job', 'Or he is alone and has no one to talk to", 'maybe he had a breakup or divorce recently, 'or maybe he was high on weed', Sam's mind was abuzz with all these thoughts, but the last statement "you were seeking something and more than you, something was seeking you", hit him hard.

Sam thought maybe this is the way all crazy people talk and rubbished the thought. "Where have we reached by the way? It has been an hour since we started. I did not switch on the GPS, thinking you know the way", Sam tried to change the conversation.

"I think we are close to Devprayag. We still have over 200 km to go. It is going to be a long journey I believe", Anand said.

"And how far is your power plant from here?", Sam asked.

"It is actually 30 km before Badrinath. I will get down on the road and then it is another 10 km inside. You can not drive there. A small trail of a mud road is the only way in and out. It is used by heavy commercial vehicles. But it is alright. I am used to walking in hills", Anand replied.

"So, you stay here alone or with family?"Sam wanted to know more about Anand.

"I am not married yet, brother", Anand replied, chuckling.

"Now I got it. Ok, do you have a girlfriend?", Sam probed further.

"No way. In this region, you hardly meet people, and no girl won't even look at someone like me", Anand started laughing.

"So that is why you talk about all that illusion, reality, purpose and bullshit. Dude, I think you need a girl in your life who will show the reality and bring you out of your illusion. I was wondering earlier, this man seems to be sick of his wife so much he started contemplating about his purpose and reality and all that stuff", Sam laughed so hard that he almost lost control over the steering wheel.

Anand looked at him and started smiling. "So, are you married if I may ask you", Anand asked hesitatingly.

"It's alright. I was married once, got divorced and now very much single. Do you think, had I been married, I could have come here alone and sitting with you", Sam said and winked at Anand.

"Oh, I am sorry", Anand apologised.

"Chill dude. Nothing to be sorry about. I am happy now and I am enjoying this trip more than anything", Sam said.

It was 10 AM but there was no sign of the Sun. Weather in these regions can change in the blink of an eye. There was a little drizzle on the way back a few minutes ago. Sam though did not worry much but getting stranded was a thought he was most scared of.

Traffic movement was getting slower as they drove further. There was a sudden downpour just after they crossed Devprayag. The road was narrow, and visibility was almost zero. A little rain also feels heavy on hills and this was a heavy downpour. The entire traffic came to a standstill. A serpentine queue started forming on the narrow road. Raindrops were sounding as if someone was throwing a barrage of heavy rocks.

The road was getting slippery, and water was coming with force from the hillside and going downhill through the road. Many small waterfalls had formed and water was gushing on the road. There was nowhere to go, not a single inch could be moved.

"Is this normal"? Sam asked Anand in a worrying tone.

"What? The rains or the weather?", Anand chuckled.

"Both", Sam said while looking at the fast-moving wiper on the windscreen of his car.

"Both are normal. Just stay tight. My only worry is a landslide. If that happens, we are badly screwed up", Anand replied trying to look calm and saw uphill outside the car window.

"The road was cleared last week. There was a serious landslide, not here though. But these roads are susceptible to landslides. It can happen anytime, anywhere and when it does, we are at the mercy of the gods", Anand added.

"Dude, are you scaring me or consoling me? This is normal but landslides are also normal. What kind of fucked up place is this?", Sam looked at Anand irritatingly.

"You signed up for this. Didn't you?", Anand looked at Sam, leaned back, put his arms around his head and took a deep breath.

"How can you be so calm? My ass is on fire here. What if water gushes inside the car? What if there is a landslide?", Sam panicked.

"So many what ifs. Let us see what happens. Welcome to the Himalayas", Anand smiled and closed his eyes.

Sam seemed visibly frustrated and started looking out from the window.

They waited for almost an hour and the rains stopped after creating enough havoc in Sam's mind.

***

Traffic had started moving but with a snail pace. This reminded Sam of Delhi's traffic.

"Where is everyone going? I thought, there will be less traffic here, but traffic jams seem to be a universal problem", Sam said following a truck in front of him.

"Traffic here is worse. In cities, you have traffic signals, and everyone goes back to their home at night and the roads are empty, but here, there is no such thing as traffic signals or going back home. Once there is a traffic jam, sometimes it goes on for days", Anand said, opening his eyes and yawning.

"Days! Are you crazy? How do people live here? Traffic jams for days! Man, that's ridiculous. I am not coming here again", Sam was amused. Anand started laughing.

They kept on driving like this for another 2 hours. The Next stop was Rudraprayag.

Rudraprayag is a town and a municipality in Rudraprayag district in the Indian state of Uttarakhand. Rudraprayag is one of the Panch Prayag of Alaknanda River, the point of confluence of rivers Alaknanda and Mandakini. Kedarnath, a Hindu holy town is located 86 km from Rudraprayag.

"Let's stop here. I am damn hungry", Sam said.

I was about to say this. You read my mind buddy. High five!", Anand said.

There was a roadside food court. Sam parked his car there and both got down. It was freezing cold outside, and the winds were not helping either. It was still drizzling, and each drop was feeling like a bullet.

They both ran inside the foot court and found a shed to stand. Sam was in disbelief seeing the crowd. Last time, he saw this much crowd at Haldiram in Connaught Place.

"You can keep people out of Delhi but can not take Delhi out of people", He murmured. Anand looked at him, smiled and said, "I agree with you, buddy".

Sam was looking around. He looked at Anand and asked, "What do you think these people are doing here? What is their purpose? Are they here like me, escaping from the summer heat or finding refuge in Lord Shiva's feet?"

"Purpose is a very big word, Sam. You won't even think about it, if the time is not right. It takes thousands of births just to even think of the word purpose. It can take many thousand births to actually realise your purpose. It is not like hot tea, when you want it, you make it and drink it. And let me tell you, when this word 'purpose' actually hits you, you are a completely different person. And that real & illusion stuff I said, you will see clearly what I meant. Until then, it is just a word from the English dictionary", Anand said, shivering in the cold.

Sam was shivering too and was in no mood to counter Anand or ask any further. He had now understood, Anand was in a different zone altogether.

Maybe staying single and alone for so long had taken his senses away and he is just one touch away from a beautiful girl to realise his true purpose.

Sam asked Anand if he would like to have tea. Anand nodded in agreement and Sam ordered two cups of tea.

Sam looked beyond the food court. The view was breathtaking. Huge mountains seemed to hug each other. Raindrops looked like white pearls, resting on the leaves of the trees around. The wind made a sound that resembled coming from a flute. Nature was majestic in its own way.

Sam knew he may not come here again so he wanted to enjoy each moment rather than frowning upon the little challenges coming his way. He knew very well; Anand was the best thing that happened to him on this trip. Without him, he would have lost interest long back and returned to Delhi.

***

After finishing the tea, they both resumed their journey. Badrinath was still well over 150 km away. The weather was looking gloomy and dark black clouds were hovering. Hence, the situation was looking very grim.

Sam was wary of a landslide that could derail everything. There was no lodge or hotel in sight and the road was getting steeper from now on. One had to be very careful to drive now. Sam was getting tired. He had not anticipated all or any of this. He had imagined a smooth road trip but rains played spoilsport.

There was absolute silence in the car. Anand was taking a nap and Sam was also feeling drowsy. Taking a halt was out of the question and traffic was moving at a snail's pace.

Sam kept on driving for another 2 hours. It was around 2 pm when he reached a small hill town, Gopeshwar. He checked with Anand if they should stop there. Anand suggested they continue the journey as they could reach Badrinath in another 3-4 hours. Sam continued driving.

They had driven hardly 20 km far from Gopeshwar, and it started to snow. At first, it looked beautiful to see snow flakes flying in the air, but soon Sam realised it is a bigger problem than rain. Snowfall makes roads slippery and can cause vehicles to slip on the road and driving conditions will be unbearable. Sam continued to drive slowly. After driving for 30 minutes, they heard a thundering sound ahead. It did not seem to come from very far off. Anand jumped off the seat and woke up with a shock.

"What happened? Are we alive?", He shouted, rubbing his eyes.

"As of now, yes", Sam answered, trying to make sense of what he heard. Entire traffic had stopped suddenly.

Anand got down from the car and walked a few metres ahead. He was trying to know what that sound was. He came back and told Sam, there was a landslide just a km ahead and the entire road had caved in.

"Fuck! No", Sam shouted. "This can't be. What do we do now? How long will it take to clear the road? He asked Anand, almost crying.

"I don't know but it gets generally cleared within 24 hours. We have no option but to wait in the car", Anand replied consoling him.

Sam put his head in his arms and banged the steering wheels with his right hand. He was scared and angry.

Anand sat in the car. He asked Sam if he wants to sleep for some time as they may have to wait for a long time.

Sam did not say anything. He went in the back seat, lied down there and closed his eyes. He was visibly tired and was soon in the grip of sleep.

Anand too leaned back and closed his eyes.

"So, you are finally here". A voice woke Sam up. Sam looked around. He was not in the car. He was at the same place, where he saw the old man for the first time in his dream.

"Who are you?", Sam asked. "What do you mean, I am finally here?".

The old man smiled, looked at Sam with the same red, hot, fiery gaze that Sam could never forget and spoke in a heavy voice, "Am I, not the reason you are here? Haven't you travelled this far to seek me? I am your purpose Samrat. I am your reality".

Having said this, the old man started laughing hysterically. Sam was dumbfounded. He was not able to move his hands and legs nor utter a word as if he was paralyzed. He wanted to call out Anand, but he was nowhere in sight. Sam gathered his full strength and shouted ANAND.

"Hey, what happened? Are you alright?", Anand was trying to wake Sam up.

Sam was dreaming. He woke up with his eyes wide open. His heart was beating like a train. He was sweating profusely.

"Where are we?", Sam asked, gasping.

"What do you mean, where are we? We were at the same place for the last 3 hours. You had been sleeping and suddenly started shouting my name in the sleep. So, I woke you up. I got scared thinking the poor man had to see so much misery in just one day.", Anand told Sam.

"Bad dream?", Anand asked.

"Not exactly. Random dream", Sam ignored the question and took a sip of the water. He looked outside.

Sun usually sets early in the hills. Night had already fallen. A handful of car's headlights were switched on as everyone wanted to save fuel & battery. One can get stuck for a couple of days in the worst case and running out of fuel or a dead battery was the last thing they wanted as trouble.

"Sam got out of the car and walked a few steps ahead. He spoke to a few guys ahead and came back.

"Did you get to know anything?", Anand asked.

"Someone was saying road repair work has already started. But it might take the entire night and the next day as well depending on the weather conditions". Sam sighed.

"They usually clear the road within 24 hours", Anand said.

"I hope so. Fingers crossed", Sam said and came inside the car and sat in the back seat.

"What if the weather conditions get worse further?", Sam asked. "What if the snowfall doesn't stop? There is another landslide. We don't even have enough water and food to survive for long. Sam was seemingly worried.

"Dude, relax! We are not stuck in a forest. This is a state highway. Stay positive. It does not take that long. And in the worst case, we can always hike to the nearest town" Anand said.

"Are you out of your mind? Hiking in this weather! Never", Sam interrupted Anand.

"I said in the worst case", Anand corrected.

"Whatever", Sam smirked.

It was 9 PM. There was absolute darkness outside except the headlights of a few cars trying to glaze through it.

Sam opened the window. There was no sound whatsoever. Most of the people were sleeping or were inside their cars. It was still snowing, and a thick blanket of snow had appeared everywhere. Everything was covered in thick white snow. It was windy and very chilly. He closed off the window. He was wondering how things unfolded since he started this journey. What led him to this place and in this situation? A lot of contemplation was brewing inside. Did he do the right thing, or was it the biggest mistake of his life? He remembered sitting in the Engage lounge a week back and drinking whiskey.

Sam made himself comfortable in the back seat, he put his hands in the pockets of his jacket. He covered his head with his jacket's hoodie. The thought of whiskey gave him an imaginary warmth. Sam soon slept. The storm of so many thoughts with so much happening in one day was not enough for him to absorb all at once.

***

Sam woke up with a big thud sound. He opened his eyes and looked outside to take the sticks of things. But the entire car was covered in snow. He opened the car door and walked outside. To his surprise, he saw only a handful of cars outside. And a few travellers in small groups walking on foot up ahead leaving their cars parked at the side of the road.

"Where did everyone disappear overnight and where is everyone going to?", he started wondering. He went ahead and asked a lady who was part of a walking group but was barely able to keep up.

"Excuse me! Where are you guys walking to? And why walk?" He inquired.

"Our car battery died. It is not starting. Our tour guide is with us. He said, there is a small village nearby, we can go there, stay, and eat food and he will come back to get the car if the road clears. But we cannot stay here now. It is getting unbearable to stay inside the car and we have small kids also with us". The lady replied anxiously.

Sam went back to the car and tried to wake Anand up.

"Hey buddy. Get up. We have a situation here. Anand woke up with his eyes half closed. He looked at Sam and asked, "What happened? Is the road clear now? You seem to have woken up for a long time now".

"I got up with a loud thud sound. I came out to check and found an almost empty road. Where is everyone going? Any idea?", Sam said in one breath.

"Leaving already? Their car battery would have died. This is common. If we stay here for long, it can happen to us too. Maybe, our battery is already dead", Anand said.

"No way. let me check", Sam put the car key in the ignition and tried to start the car. The engine made a cranking sound, but nothing happened. Sam tried again but the battery was dead indeed.

"What now?", Sam looked at Anand worried with a pale face.

"I warned you in Rishikesh. Didn't I", Anand said.

"We are not in Rishikesh. The risk was mine and I told so. Just tell me, what do we do now?", Sam was furious and irritated.

Almost all the cars were stranded, and a few had left last night. They took a U-turn and went back.

"We can also hike to the nearest town. It is not far. But it will take at least 2-3 hours in this weather", Anand proposed.

"Do you know the way? And what if the weather gets worse and we get stranded on the way? And in the worst case, what if there is a landslide on the way?", Sam had his own doubts.

"We don't have much of a choice here dude", Anand interrupted him. "Now when almost everyone has left, we are left to fend off ourselves. If we stay here further, we may be in deeper trouble".

Sam looked at Anand helplessly and then looked around. There were empty cars covered in snow. The weather was still not clear. A lot of people had left early in the morning. It was 9 AM.

"Let's start then if this is the only option left", Sam sighed and got out of the car. He picked up his backpack, put some essential stuff from another bag in it, locked the car, gave it a long look and asked Anand to come out. Sam locked the car and they both started to hike in the direction where everywhere else went.

***

There was a small trail from the main road going uphill. This is the track everyone took to leave for the town. There was no one on that trail. Footsteps from the previous group had fainted due to continuous snowfall. Anand was walking in the front and Sam was following him. It was windy and chilly, and snowfall was adding to the already worsened conditions.

However, Sam had never set foot on snow before, so he was seemingly excited in the beginning. He was making snowballs and throwing them at Anand, who did not seem to care. He was focused on walking.

It was a narrow trail, completely covered in thick snow. There were a few trees on either side. The weather was still not clear and there was still no sign of the Sun. Sam looked back. He had a heavy heart leaving behind his car.

"Hey Anand", he asked. "What if I don't get to see my car when we get back here?"

"Who will take it from here and why?", Anand turned around and responded panting.

"What do you mean who will take and why?", Sam wondered and walked a little faster to catch up with Anand.

"It's simple dude. I can understand that you are worried about your car's safety but leaving a car on the road like this and coming back for it later is very common here. So, relax, you won't find even a single tyre missing", Anand winked.

Sam gave Anand a disgusted look and kept on walking. It was not an easy route. There was no road. The trail they were following, was a natural trail made by continuous usage of that stretch to reach the town. But the snow had covered it and was hardly visible except for the foot marks left by earlier hikers and travellers who took the same trail early in the morning. But the footmarks were getting frail, and the trail was hardly visible. Continuous snowfall was making the matter worse; hence the hike was getting treacherous slowly.

Sam was just following Anand, thinking he knew the way. Anand too was not sure about the way any more than Sam, but he did not let Sam know about it. He knew Sam would panic and would create a scene as it was his idea to hike for the town. So, he kept mum and continued to follow the trail.

The weather was getting worse slowly. Snow was getting thicker, and the hike was becoming steeper with every step. Although Sam and Anand were wearing fur jackets, the wind was feeling like snow arrows, piercing from all directions.

Snowfall had intensified. There was no escape from it. High wind speed, heavy snowfall, treacherous trail and steep hike, it could have been a perfect death wish but today, no one wished for it. Their legs were getting heavier with each step they took, their hands becoming numb and their breath becoming weak.

Snowfall further intensified and nothing was visible now. Anand was hardly a few feet ahead, but Sam was not able to keep up and see him. Dark clouds had completely taken over the sky and the Sun.

Sam had never imagined, one day he would find himself in such a situation. He called Anand, but his voice drowned in the sound of the wind. Anand was trying to keep his feet intact and move ahead. The visibility was getting obstructed due to heavy snowfall.

This was a rugged trail and every step needed to be taken with utmost care. Sam was not able to see Anand clearly. He could only guess him as a colourful vague figure moving in front of him. He tried to call Anand a few times but to no avail. He was getting short of breath. His legs were trembling. He was hardly able to move. Every small step seemed like an uphill task. Sam was using his full force, but his body was giving in. The brutal force of nature was in beast mode.

Sam was not even able to move an inch ahead. He sat where he was. He could see a colourful figure moving ahead and fading away slowly in the thick blanket of snow. He called for Anand again, but his voice was again lost in the sound of heavy wind. He held his head from both his hands.

Sam was now on his own. Hundreds of miles away from the comfort of his home. He thought of Rohit, his friends, his parents and everyone else he liked being with. He tried one last time to call Anand. His voice had fainted by now and he could hardly speak.

Sam fell on the ice. He took his mobile out of his pocket. There was no signal and the battery was counting its last breath. . His heart was beating very fast as he had no idea what to do. He was losing consciousness as his vision became blurr and his speech was getting impaired. He remembered the day he was standing on his balcony and saw that old man in the empty land in front of his apartment.

Tears rolled from his eyes. He was now repenting the decision to come here and started to curse Anand.

"Moron", he murmured in a frail voice. Sam recollected his entire strength and stood up on his feet. He did not want to die lying there. Visibility due to the snowstorm had worsened further. The trail he was walking upon had disappeared and it was all white ocean of ice everywhere. Sam was clueless about the direction. He looked around. There was no sign of a human being.

His best guess was to move straight up. However, he had hardly any strength left in him, but Sam knew, if he gave up, he may not survive these conditions. He started to walk uphill.

Snowstorms and landslides are common events in this weather in that region. Therefore, it is highly recommended to be accompanied by a local guide at such places.

"Where the fuck are you man?", Sam shouted trying to walk and look straight. He thought if he continued to walk, he might catch Anand on the way. Anand might have taken shelter somewhere nearby as hiking in this weather was impossible. There were a lot of stray rocks on the way but not big enough for a shelter. And standing under a tree was as good as being in the open.

The ground under the feet on hills can be deceiving. It might look all rocky and sturdy but if there are cracks and if covered with snow, it can cave in with little weight.

Sam discovered this phenomenon soon. There was a small ditch in front of him and he jumped to cross over to the other side, but he slipped as the ground under his feet caved in. His head hit the rock and he fell into the ditch. His forehead was wounded, and it started to bleed, not profusely though. It was like a double whammy now. Although the ditch was not very deep, it seemed gigantic giving Sam's wound and already broken morale.

Sam tried to get up but felt too weak and the pain was excruciating. He took the support of the side walls of the ditch and tried to get up. He was not aware of his bleeding. He stood up and came out of the ditch. His backpack had also fallen in the ditch while he fell in it. He went back to the ditch to pick it up and while he leaned forward, a small drop of blood fell on the backpack. Shocked as he was, he put his hand on his forehead to check and was in for a rude shock. He started panicking seeing the blood.

"What the fuck", Sam shouted. He rubbed the forehead from his palm and was relieved to see the bleeding was not a lot. It was a small cut and had dried quickly by the cold winds. He collected his backpack and came out of the ditch.

Sam was getting physically weak, but this sudden accident enraged him. He had always been in control of the things around him and after a long time, he felt as if he was at the mercy of nature. This thought gave him a strange and adrenaline rush.

His legs were still trembling, and the wind was piercing like nails, but Sam had got a renewed motivation.

"I am not dying today, not here at least", he said to himself and started walking uphill.

Sam continued to hike for another half an hour. His lips were parched, and his stomach was making sounds. He was hungry but had nothing to eat. Sam ignored it and kept on hiking up.

Suddenly he chanced upon a big rock on one side that had its top curved down, giving it a look of a wave frozen in time. But there was some space in it that Sam could use as shelter.

Sam sat there. He looked around. It was utter wilderness, with no living being in sight. The wind was making whistling sounds and trees were dancing with the high wind speed. Sam bent his head backwards and took the support of the rock and closed his eyes. A flurry of thoughts crossed his mind like a flash. His childhood, college memories, first job, first love, first business venture, failures, marriage, divorce, and at last his current trip.

Sam was very tired and was soon in the grip of sleep.

"Done already?", a deep and heavy voice paused his train of thoughts. "So, this is all you got. I thought you were seeking me, but here you are. Lying like a lifeless corpse. A little difficulty and you gave up already. I thought you were the one, but I was mistaken".

Sam opened his eyes hurriedly, shook his head and looked around frantically. There was no sign of anyone. He thought he was dreaming. He checked his phone again. The battery had died completely. Sam wanted to rest there and wait for the snowstorm to get over. However, the storm seemed to get even more intense. It was around 1 PM but looked like late evening as Sun god seemed to be kidnapped by dark black clouds.

Hunger, parched lips, thirst, weak body, wounded head and sleep was making Sam feel miserable. He heard the sound of someone laughing but it was too feeble. He then heard someone whispering in his ear from behind. He turned around to see but there was none. Sam was hallucinating. He was finding it difficult to separate reality from illusion. Sam was convinced this was his last day.. He felt the warmth of the tears. But they dried the instant they came out of the eyes.

Sam folded his hands with closed eyes and started crying like a baby. "I am sorry Mummy and Papa", he kept repeating while crying. His voice was becoming feeble slowly and his body was shivering.

Suddenly the wailing stopped. There was absolute silence. Sam was lying there still. There was no movement in his body. His head was bent backwards, eyes closed, and lips opened. There were fresh warm tears still in the eyes and a drop of them fell on his cheek and froze.

Sam was finally at peace. His heart was not beating anymore. His sufferings had ended.

# CHAPTER 18

## *The Separation*

**5th June 2018**

Anand looked behind. He suddenly realised; he did not start this journey alone. He could not find Sam following him. He shouted his name. There was no response. He had come very far off now and all this while, he thought Sam was right behind him without realising Sam had lost his way long back.

The snowstorm had subsided a bit now, but the Sun was still playing hide and seek. Anand decided to go back and look for Sam. He himself was tired but the thought of Sam wandering away gave him chills. It was his idea to hike, and Sam was gracious enough to follow him and moreover, it was Sam who offered him the lift.

"What did I do? I Should have rested or looked behind earlier." Anand said in a wailed voice. "Where do I find you now?"

Anand started to hike down shouting Sam's name. Sam was nowhere to be found. He followed the same trail he took to come uphill in the hope of finding Sam or any footmarks. But there were none.

Anand shouted Sam's name frantically in all directions. He had not even exchanged his mobile number with Sam. But that was anyway useless as there was no mobile network.

He kept going downhill, but it was an ocean of snow everywhere. Broken branches and fallen trees were the only company he had. He had no idea where to go and going back down to the main road where they had started was not a good idea either.

Anand sat over a fallen tree. He was trying to catch his breath. He was in a dilemma whether to walk down further and search for Sam or continue to hike up and reach the town. He sat for a few minutes and then got up with a heavy heart. He decided to come back with more people and search for him. Of course, he did not want to leave Sam dying there in that wilderness for a certain death.

***

# CHAPTER 19

## *The Ordeal Begins*

**8th June 2018**

The sun was brightly lit, and it was a hot summer day. A man with lean figure, with a small piece of cloth wrapped around his waist, was walking through a forest, carrying a bucket full of water from a stream nearby. He was sweating profusely and was not able to balance himself. He was going uphill through the forest. He was stopping after every few steps to catch his breath and then resume again.

He finally climbed the hill and crossed the forest. He was moving towards a small, dilapidated Hut made of bamboo trees. He put the bucket down at the entrance, opened the door and went inside.

A wounded man was lying on the floor, he poured some water in his mouth, wiped his face and hands and sat next to him. The sun was right above the hut. It had been raining for the last few days and water was still seeping through it. So, water droplets and sunlight were directly falling over the face of that wounded man. He opened his eyes partially and moaned with pain.

His vision was blurry. He was not able to make sense of his surroundings. He tried to get up, but his body was too weak. The old man gestured to him to keep lying down. He asked him in a feeble voice, "Where am I? Who are you?"

"Oh, so you are finally awake. You have been sleeping for three days now. Don't get up. You seem to be very weak. I was not sure if you will survive. My name is Bhaskar", that man replied.

"3 days! What are you saying? I have been here for the last three days! Where did you find me? What happened to me?" that wounded man asked in shock, writhing in pain.

Bhaskar gave him a serious stare for a few seconds and that made that wounded man more anxious. Bhaskar then asked him, "What were you doing there? You were lying unconscious, not very far from here. Had I not seen you, you would have been dead by now, and some vultures have been feeding off your corpse by now".

These words, almost spoken in a cold tone, gave chills down the spine of that wounded man. He was shocked to hear this. He had tears in his eyes. He was looking at his surroundings and could see the forest from the window and hear the sound of birds chirping. He then asked Bhaskar." Where am I now?".

"We are in Dungra village", Bhaskar replied.

"How far off is this place from Badrinath?", the wounded man asked.

"Badrinath is very far off from here but you first tell me, why were you there? And were you alone or with someone else?", Bhaskar asked.

That wounded man sighed and said," Why was I there? It's a long story. And did you find just me or anyone else too?"

"Just you. Why? Were you with someone?", Bhaskar asked again.

The wounded man's face turned red with rage. He turned his head sideways and replied, "NO. I was alone".

"Do you have a name?", Bhaskar asked.

"My name is Sam", that wounded man replied.

***

# CHAPTER 20

## The Agony

**8th June 2018**

Sam could not believe he was there for 3 days, lying unconscious in that hut. He was cursing Anand for leaving him there to die. He was not able to come to terms with all the misfortune that suddenly had fallen on him. this entire trip seemed to be jinxed to him.

His entire body was aching. His feet were swollen and his hands felt too heavy to even lift an inch up. He looked around to see his backpack. It was lying in a corner. He requested Bhaskar to pass that backpack to him. Bhaskar leaned forward to hand over the bagpack to Sam, but Sam literally snatched the backpack from Bhaskar. He was looking for his phone and other stuff. Everything was intact as it is.

Sam looked at Bhaskar with a look of gratitude, held his backpack closer to him and lied down.

Bhaskar left the hut soon after. Sam could see him walking away and vanishing in the forest. It was afternoon. There was no way to know the exact time of the day as Sam's watch was not working, probably it gave away in the extreme cold.

Sam was too tired and weak. He had been unconscious for 3 days and had not eaten anything either. He was lying there in disbelief. His mind was not able to believe all this.

Sam thought, maybe he was dreaming. Maybe he fell asleep in his car. Sam pinched his arm to check if he was dreaming. But the reality struck him very hard. It was all real. He was far away from anything that he could consider as a civilization.

Sam had never imagined himself to be in such a situation. His idea of an adventurous trip had badly backfired now. He started to think about his friends, family and office colleagues. It had been 4 days since he was missing. Missing was the right word as his mobile phone was also switched off for the last 4 days.

"Everyone will be trying to reach me. What will my parents be going through? They have no idea, their son is the biggest idiot who almost got himself killed, lying wounded in a goddamn hut hundreds of miles away from civilization all alone", Sam was talking to himself. He was angry at himself for trusting Anand.

"Bloody asshole! He did not even look behind to check if I was there or not. How stupid can you be Sam? How can you trust someone like this? What if he had hit me and ran away with all my valuables", Sam muttered.

Sam was hungry and there was nothing to eat in that Hut. Bhaskar was also nowhere in sight and Sam was too weak to get up. He gathered his strength and tried to get up. There was a sharp pain in both his legs. He somehow got up and looked outside the window. There was nothing but creepy silence everywhere.

That Hut was standing alone in that forest. Now more than his hunger, Sam was worried about the hunger of wild animals. He had survived the snowstorm and the thought of being eaten by a wild animal gave him shivers down his spine.

"You need to get out of here Sam. You cannot stay here and die. This entire trip has been a curse it seems", Sam told himself.

Sam was in his thoughts and then saw Bhaskar walking towards the Hut.

Bhaskar entered the Hut and saw Sam sitting on the floor.

"Hungry?", Bhaskar asked.

Sam nodded his head meaning yes. Bhaskar had brought some bananas from the forest, and he offered them to Sam. There were many firsts in Sam's life now in the last 5 days.

Sam peeled off the bananas like a child and quickly hogged onto them. He was famished. He finished 6 bananas in a jiffy.

"What do you do? Where are you from?", Bhaskar asked Sam.

"What do I do? Sam repeated the question for himself, "I work in an IT company. I stay in Delhi. But how will you know what IT is", Sam said and dismissed the answer in a whispering tone.

"By the way, what are you doing here in this wilderness? You stay here all alone?" Sam asked him.

"I know what IT is. And this may be wilderness for you but for me, it is my home", Bhaskar replied in a serious tone as if telling Sam, he is the outsider here.

Bhaskar looked outside and told Sam, "Listen! I need to go to some place and I shall leave now. You should stay here. Do not try to leave this place on your own, although I know, you want to do that desperately. You are too weak to travel right now and this forest is full of wild animals. So don't venture out for even a stroll. When gain some strength, I shall myself take you to the nearest town".

Sam had his mouth wide open. He asked in shock, "What do you mean, I cannot go out? Are you telling me, I will stay here for the next few days? And who are you to decide what I should do? I am thankful you saved my life, but I really can't stay here. I have my family and friends waiting for me in Delhi. If I don't call them or go back soon, they will be worried.

Sam was in no mood to relent or follow Bhaskar's advice.

Sam tried to get up but felt acute pain and stumbled. Bhaskar held Sam with his arm, supported him and asked him to sit on the floor. Sam was moaning in pain and sat on the floor.

"Now you understand, what did I mean?", Bhaskar asked.

Sam said nothing but turned his head sideways and said, "Go! Leave this place right away. I don't need anyone. What is wrong with people? They just come into life and leave you to die. That asshole Anand left me to die there in a snowstorm and now you are also leaving. Just leave!", Sam shouted.

He had tears in his eyes. Bhaskar stood up, looked at Sam and walked out of the hut.

Sun had started to set. The chirping sound of birds had been replaced with the chirping of crickets. Bhasksr had closed the bamboo door of the hut while he walked out.

It was completely dark in the hut and outside, but the fireflies were trying to fight hard with the dark shadows of night. The temperature had also fallen sharply. Weather changes in the hills very quickly.

Sam was shivering with cold inside the hut. Due to the cold, his pain had also increased. It was going to be a long and difficult night. The howling of wolves and wild dogs could be heard from any distance in the eerie silence.

Sometimes, the wind made a howling sound so loud it felt like a wolf howling in the bushes nearby the hut. Sam was trying to sleep but it was miles away from his eyes tonight.

He never felt this scared in his lifetime. Alone in a forest, fighting the extreme cold, wounded, unable to walk, hungry, surrounded by wild animals and only saviour, a dilapidated bamboo hut.

"Why are you doing this, God? What have I done to go through all this? I should have died on that cliff. You saved me to go through another hell as if that was not enough. I don't know if I shall survive another night or not, but I know one thing for sure, my belief in you is shattering fast", Sam shouted in anger and punched his fist on the floor.

This was the longest night of Sam's life. He was tired and wounded and wanted to sleep but the darkness, the fear of the unknown, the cold and hunger kept him awake.

***

The sound of the chirping of the birds and the blazing sun woke Sam up. He had no memory of when he fell asleep. And now, the Sun was right above the hut.

Bhaskar had not returned yet and Sam was thirsty. He looked around to see if there was any vessel. Yesterday, Bhaskar had left a bucket of water in the hut. Sam reached out to it and drank some water. His pain had subsided to some extent, but he was still not well to walk for a long distance.

He came out of the hut and looked around. The first time, he got the full view of that place in the last 5 days since he was brought there by Bhaskar.

That hut was basically in the middle of nowhere. There was a thick cover of forest all around and it seemed as if he was on top of a hill. He could hear the sound of a river stream down the hill. The hut itself seemed not more than a few bamboos put together for a shelter. Sam took a deep breath and sat on a rock beside the hut.

He reached out in his pocket to look for his mobile which had been dead for 5 days now. He was sitting in complete silence in that wilderness, hungry and clueless.

A lot of things were playing in Sam's mind. How he got into this situation was something he was not able to comprehend.

It all seemed like a destiny to him. The sightings of that old man in Delhi, weird dreams, the documentary, the book in the bookstore, all transpired him to plan this trip. Meeting Anand was a coincidence but believing him was his conscious choice which he felt was hasty though.

"What other options did I have? Had I not listened to him for the hiking after we had stuck, I might have been in deeper trouble, maybe. But what if the rescue team had arrived? Here, there is no chance or any hope for anyone to even notice me. I am sitting here, all alone, deep inside a forest with no sight of civilization", Sam was talking to himself with teary eyes.

He had no idea about the time of the day. He thought, Bhaskar might be coming anytime and he kept sitting outside, waiting for him. There was little water left in the bucket and was not enough to survive another hot day.

***

Sam sat and waited there for many hours. Bhaskar had gone for many hours now and not yet returned. Sam was hungry and the water bucket was also empty.

Sam decided to take a stroll in the forest and look for some fruits and water. He went inside the hut and picked up the bucket. He did not have a lot of strength and was limping too, but the pain had subsided significantly.

Sam got up and walked away from the hut towards a bushy area leading to the forest.

The land around the hut was muddy due to the rains last night and water had accumulated at some place in small pits. Sam had to be careful as he did not want another trouble on top of whatever had already happened.

There was no trail, so he had to find his own way around those mud-filled holes.

He walked a little inside the forest. The trees were thick and did not allow much sunlight to penetrate through them. So, the visibility and temperature, were significantly lesser than around the hut.

Now the problem was, Sam had no idea which fruit to be picked up. In his regular life, he purchased fruits from supermarkets, wrapped up in plastic or in beautiful boxes, all shining with price stickers on them. But here, everything looked so different. Life in the wild can be merciless and unforgiving. Sam now remembered how much he hated watching the discovery channel.

"If only you had taken little interest in watching Discovery channel, it could have been much better, you moron", Sam told himself in frustration.

The rain last night had caused havoc in the forest with many mutilated and uprooted trees all over the place.

Sometimes, there is a silver lining in every cloud, and this proved to be absolutely true that day. Blackberry is a common fruit found in forests. And it was all over the place. Sam could recognise it well as in his childhood, it used to be one of his favourite fruits. He picked up as much as he could and put them in his jacket and pockets of his trousers.

The next challenge was to find potable water. Rains last night, however, had made the entire area wet but there was no way to collect the water except from the small pits. Sam had no option; he was tired, and his body was giving up too. He collected some water from a pit in the bucket and returned to the hut.

***

Sam was tired so he went inside the hut. Sun was hiding behind the clouds that had invaded the sky surprisingly. The weather was turning bad and high winds had started. Sam had returned just in time.

He sat on the floor and drank some water from the bucket. He picked up some berries and ate them.

This was the first time in the last 5-6 days he ate something. He closed his eyes when he ate the first few berries. It was a different experience. He had never gone hungry for so many days ever in his life so eating those berries seemed like the best meal of his life.

He opened his eyes, took a deep breath and told himself, "Where has life taken me to?". He laid down on the floor and closed his eyes. He was soon in the grip of sleep.

While asleep, Sam felt as if someone entered the room. He opened his eyes and tried to see in pitch darkness. He shouted, "Who is there?". But there was no response.

"He moved his hands around him to see if it hit someone but there was nothing he could touch.

His biggest fear of being eaten alive by a wild animal had taken over him completely and he decided to stay awake.

He checked the door, and it was closed. However, the window had no doors or any means to close it. He could hear the sound of heavy winds and drizzle. But he was also certain, it was not an animal but a human who might have entered the hut from the window.

Sam kept guarding the window the entire night and slept only when the sun's rays lit the hut.

The next day, Sam woke up to the sounds of thunder of the clouds. He had been sleeping for a long time. He quickly reached out to the water bucket and the stock of berries. Both were in scant quantities, insufficient to last long.

It had started to rain again, and water had been leaking from the roof of the hut. Sam got up and sat in a corner and bundled himself. He looked outside the window. The trees were violently moving in all directions due to heavy winds and the rains were so heavy, it looked as if a cloud had burst right above the hut.

A flurry of thoughts crossed his mind. What if he dies here or could never go back to his home or could never see his family and friends again? What if he gets stranded in this place forever? These thoughts made him feel morbid and his head started spinning. He closed his eyes and sat there.

The smell of wet mud, flowers and the sound of rain is a beautiful experience when you have a roof over your head, and when you are socially, financially, physically & emotionally secure but it all looks like a harrowing experience when you are wounded and stranded in a forest full of wild animals, hundreds of miles away from any civilization. Sam was aghast at everything. Nothing made him feel better. He was helpless, clueless and without help.

# CHAPTER 21

## *The Truth*

**10th June 2018**

Sam slept quickly in that corner while the rains wreaked havoc. In his dreams, he saw he was being rescued and he reached Delhi safely.

He called his family who looked seemingly worried. His father had filed a missing person complaint which led to his discovery in that forest.

He called his friends who too were worried as hell. He was happy to be back and was waiting to be united with his loved ones. He was waiting at his home for his friends to come over and see him.

"Hey dude. Welcome back.", Rohit called Sam on his mobile, "I am so happy that you are back. I was so damn worried. In Fact, we all were. Shilpa, Jack, me and Shakti, would talk about you every day in the office. I guess, there is a lot we want to hear. Ok, listen, we shall come over on the weekend to see you. Since you were gone, I had to take up your projects and it is a big mess. I will tell you when we meet. And you take care of yourself and do call me if you need anything". Rohit hung up before Sam could say anything.

Sam called his father to check if he was coming to see him. But he was occupied with the registration of the new flat he had purchased last year. He also promised to come over the weekend.

Sam started to wonder if anyone missed him. He thought his family and friends would just run to see him on the first news of him being alive. But life kept everyone busy, it did not stop for anyone. It never does. And he did understand it well. It did not stop for him when he got divorced or when his mother died. So, he could certainly not expect anyone to keep thinking about him all the time or blame anyone for his misery.

Sam suddenly woke up from his dream. This sudden realisation did not make him feel sad or miserable. He, for the first time since he found himself in that forest, felt a little relieved knowing that life will never stop for anyone. He knew people will worry but they have a separate life as well to keep the show on.

He is not being missed right now, this realisation, made him suddenly feel very light, as if the monkey got off his shoulders.

Everyone is indispensable in this world. There is nothing wrong with it. Why should our loved ones stop living when someone they love dies? Isn't this the whole truth? Isn't death the last truth on the earth? Aren't we all supposed to die one day? Why do we need to bind someone with our expectations? Why should people act or think in a manner we want them to be? Why can't they choose the life they want? Why can't people be free of the bonds they live with or the burden of relationships they carry?

These thoughts were playing in Sam's mind. His pain and misery seemed to feel a little less when the world started to appear like an illusion. Everything he believed to be his own, his possession from people to objects started to feel meaningless. And exactly at that moment, he remembered the words of Anand, the purpose of life, its futility and its illusion. And now Anand's words were finally making sense to Sam.

The heavy burden of people's expectations, his expectations from the world, his desires, passions, associations, relationships, and possessions suddenly started to diminish and seemed insignificant.

The rain had stopped now but the roof of the hut was still leaking. Sam now had a renewed motivation. He got up, picked up his backpack and his dead mobile phone. He wanted to get out of that place now. He wanted to be saved not for anyone else but for himself. He wanted to live not to fulfil his dreams, aspirations or any expectations but to find the larger meaning of his life. If money and possessions could have given comfort or happiness, it was nowhere to be found today.

Sam left the hut and went in the direction where Bhaskar had ventured 2 days ago. He still had pain in his legs and his body was weak, but nothing could deter him today from leaving that place.

That entire area was completely muddy and in water due to heavy rain from early morning. Sam had expected a trail to follow but there was none to be found.

Almost everything was under the water. He stopped for a while and looked behind towards the hut. For a moment, he thought to go back and wait for the water to recede or the sun to appear, but his patience had waned. He did not want to just wait there to be rescued or die.

He started to wade through the water deep inside the forest. He did not know the way, but he remembered hearing the sound of a water stream the other day. And he knew, if he could follow down a water stream, he would find a civilization in the direction of its flow. So, Sam had to go downhill and that was not going to be easy in those climate conditions.

The path was slippery, rocky and full of small plants. The chances of being bitten by a snake or Scorpio were high.

"If I did not die until now, I am destined to live a little more", Sam murmured.

He continued to make his way through the muddy path down the hill. Visibility was not very good due to heavy clouds, still hovering above his head. It could rain any time and Sam knew that would mean disaster for him.

He had barely covered some distance down the hill, it started drizzling. There were a lot of trees around, but they were all wet due to heavy showers early in the morning, so taking shelter under a tree was not an option either.

It was just a drizzle, but the wind speed was picking up. Sam continued to walk down the hill carefully.

Suddenly, there was a very loud thunder of clouds. He lost his balance and almost fell but a tree next to him saved him and he held it tight with both his hands.

It started raining heavily as if clouds had burst right above his head. Water drops felt like stones falling from the sky. There was no place to hide. Sam tried to look around in the hope of finding a big rock or a tree where he could take shelter. But the sight of that place was full of fallen trees and broken branches.

He hurriedly tried to walk down the hill. His legs paining, the rain feeling like piercing arrows and wounded body, Sam could not have expected a worse day in his life.

Wind speed was pushing him ahead and it was getting difficult for him to stay afoot. He was not able to see anything around him and the rains were wreaking havoc again.

His leg suddenly slipped and his hold on the tree loosened. Sam tried to hold something while he started to slip down the hill, but the slippery surface was not helping either.

His grip on the tree loosened completely and he started to roll down the hill. There were many small rocks and broken trees that he hit on his way down. His body was badly bruised and started to bleed from multiple wounds.

Sam was screaming with pain, but his voice was lost in the heavy rains and wilderness and there was no one to even hear it let alone help.

It got very dark suddenly and the rains became even more incessant. If it pierced like an arrow before, it surely felt like a barrage of stones hitting hard.

Sam was holding onto a branch of a fallen tree. If he had lost his grip, he would have fallen directly into the river flowing down.

It was completely dark now; the rain had become more intense, and the wind sounded like the howling of a pack of wolves. In less than 6 days, Sam was again experiencing the dance of death.

He had closed his eyes and started to scream. It was more of frustration and anger that he wanted to vent out. He kept on screaming until his voice gave up. His tears got washed away in the rain and so did the blood from his wounds.

Sam had now lost all hopes to stay alive. No one was coming to save him, and he knew it well. His grip on the tree branch was loosening slowly and so did his strength. Sam was barely hanging there.

Sam suddenly had his entire life flashed like a movie in front of him. He saw himself as a child playing, growing up to be a boy, falling in love, first paycheque of the business he started, getting married, divorced, putting his life together and finally coming to this trip. All these memories came in a flash.

Sam's hands started to tremble. He shouted at the top of his voice, "Is this it? Is this the end" So be it" and he lost the grip of that branch and started to fall into the river.

# CHAPTER 22

## *Rebirth*

**11th June 2018**

Sam had closed his eyes. He knew this was the end.

He kept on falling towards the ground. He was ready to accept the end, finally.

Suddenly, he felt, he was not falling any further, his eyes were still closed.

He felt as if he was floating in the air. His body had become very light. He sensed a strange warmth and an intense light around him.

He thought he was dead, and this is his afterlife experience.

"Am I dead? Am I in heaven or hell? Open your eyes, idiot", Sam said to himself.

Sam slowly opened his eyes and to his utter bewilderment, he found himself floating in the air. He could hear the sound of the river below and could see the mountains around. It was still raining but no drops were falling on him. There was a bright light around him.

Sam's mouth was wide open in disbelief. He shouted, "Am I dead? What kind of joke is this?

Suddenly the bright light became a big ball of light. He could clearly see a figure emerging out of that light.

Sam was not sure if he was dead or dreaming. That figure became clearer, and it was shining like a ball of fire.

Sam rubbed his eyes and tried to see that figure. It was a bearded old man. His eyes were big and fiery red, like blazing fire. Sam's eyes & mouth became wide open. His jaw dropped. His body started to shiver. He wanted to move but could not move an inch.

"This can't be. This is not possible. I am dreaming", Sam said to himself and pinched himself. That bearded old man was floating in the air and was right in front of Sam, looking into his soul through his eyes. He was the same old man that Sam saw a few times in Delhi, at a traffic signal, near his house, in his dreams and on the cover of the book in the bookstore.

Sam was losing his mind now. He screamed, "Who are you? Am I dead? What do you want? Where did you come from?". His whole body was shaking.

The old man smiled and kept looking at Sam. His gaze could see through Sam's soul, that's how Sam felt.

Sam remembered the documentary he watched on Youtube. The description of the old man in the documentary matched exactly with the one floating in the air in front of him. Sam too kept staring at the old man. He had so many questions and too many misbeliefs, but no words could come out of his lip as if they were frozen. He wanted to move, and despite his best efforts, his body could not move an inch.

"So, you are here finally!" The old man spoke in a deep voice. The voice echoed in that valley.

This voice seemed familiar to Sam. He had heard it before. But where? He tried to recall.

"Oh yes! I know this voice. The same voice I heard in my dream. He is the same old man. I know you", Sam murmured or at least tried.

Before Sam could speak anything, the old man said in a very deep and heavy voice, slowly, "What took you so long to come here? Don't you recognize me Samrat? I had been longing to meet you. After all, you have gone through so much misery in the last few days and the tests. And you have finally succeeded".

"But who, who, who are you? And ffffirst tell me, me me, am I alive or is this a dream", Sam could finally stammer some words.

The old man laughed hard. The laughter too echoed in that valley. Sam was seeing him laughing like a mad man, "Of Course, you are alive. This is not a dream but you. What you have perceived as reality was a dream. All your sufferings, sorrow, griefs, happiness, everything was a dream. It was all in your mind. It never existed".

"I don't know what you are talking about. Are you trying to say, you are some higher power who summoned me here? I don't care who you are. And how are you and I floating in the air? Where is this light coming from?" Sam asked in absolute bewilderment.

The old man smiled, came closer to Sam and held his hand. Sam felt as if he touched a live wire. His entire body went into a trance. That experience was something he had never felt. He started to feel light. He felt no pain in his body. The tiredness had vanished.

Sam did not want to open his eyes rather he was not able to. At that moment, his agony, frustration and fears, all were gone.

"Wake up Samrat", the old man said, and, in that state, Sam opened his eyes and saw his body still floating in the air. The old man was still holding his hand. He asked the old man, "Am I dead?"

The old man replied, "Not yet but now you are born again. You have been dead all your conscious life so far."

"What does it mean?", Sam asked.

"What do you long for now? To be reunited with your family, old life, is that what you wish for now?" the old man asked.

Sam kept silent for a while. Had someone asked this question a week back, he would not have even blinked his eyes and said "Yes, ofcourse". But today was different.

"I don't know", Sam replied.

"And why not", the old man asked.

"Because I no longer feel I belong there. We all live an individual selfish life. Our sorrows, our griefs, our success, our happiness or every emotion we feel, we think it is We. But who is We?

All my life, I was chasing something, some happiness which was changing from one thing to another. Nothing in life gave me a satisfied feeling which lasted even for a few hours. The target kept changing and hence I kept chasing it. It was a wild goose chase.

Life never stops for anyone. It goes on. No one would have missed me in my old life and even if they did, they would have moved on. So, I really don't know what I will do going back to a life where you are constantly judged and need to prove your worth all the time. A life where happiness is an event, an object, an experience and not a state of mind".

"What you call old life, or the world is an illusion, Samrat. It always existed only in your thoughts", the old man said and put his hand over Sam's head.

Sam felt an excruciating pain as if his skin was being peeled and his internal organs were desperate to get separated from the body. Those few seconds felt like a lifetime. He felt as if his soul was being taken away from him. His entire life raced in front of him in a flash. All his memories of the past were fading into oblivion. His doubts, dilemmas and pain were giving way to a still mind. His body felt light. He felt ecstatic. He just did not want this experience to stop. He wanted to remain in this trance.

"Open your eyes", the old man said.

Sam tried to open his eyes, but he felt intoxicated. "I am not able to open my eyes", Sam said.

The old man shook Sam holding his arm. Sam opened his eyes as if he woke up from a deep and long sleep.

He looked at the old man and kept looking at him for a long time. There were two gazes now, looking into each other's souls, both fiery red.

"Who are you?" Sam asked the old man.

"I am thy faceless, nameless you have been seeking all your life. I am the beginning and the end", the old man replied smiling.

"And who am I?" Sam asked the old man.

"You are a seeker of me and now a part of me. You are a conduit of my work, of my purpose in this world', the old man replied without blinking his eyes and gazing into Sam's eyes.

"I am the doer, the maker and the observer. I just do my dharma. I don't control the outcome. I am a part of the universe which gets manifested through me. All human suffering is due to attachment. You get anxious when you attach your karma to its outcome. In reality, you control nothing. But when you observe this reality from the outside, you realise, it is like a movie running on the screen. You enjoy it but do not bring it home. That is how this world functions. It is a movie, enjoy it but don't become a character in it. Don't bring it home. You are home already. You gain nothing, you feel nothing, you lose nothing. I am you; you are me and everything in this world is my reflection and I see myself in everyone as we are one entity. The moment you differentiate, duality comes in and you think you are an individual and then ego takes birth and you become a character in this world and you feel you control the outcomes of your life and how other characters behave. But you are not an individual entity. You are one with the universe.", the old man explained, "And you have a purpose, Samrat".

"My purpose! What is my purpose?", Sam asked that old man.

"Each one of us has a purpose in this world. But this world is an illusion which distracts you and you start believing your purpose is to amass wealth, attach yourself to objects and indulge in sensory pleasures. There is nothing wrong with it. However, that's a play to be played and not the reality, certainly not the destination. Forgetting your purpose is certainly wrong and by the time you realise it, the time has gone already. You have suffered in this life, and you will suffer in your next and the next and this cycle will go on for eternity until in one life you break this chain and realise your purpose to not to come back to this earth and not be born again."

"And how can I realize my purpose?, Sam asked like a child.

"By knowing, you are neither this body nor a mind. Ask yourself, who am I? And one day, you will find all the answers you seek," the old man replied.

Sam was lying there listening to him without blinking his eyes. He closed his eyes and he felt intoxicated once again. He just did not want to open his eyes again. He stayed in that state for a long time.

He experienced the words said by that old man. How trivial and foolish it is to think we control what we do. In the desire for control, we end up losing what we can do well. The journey is more beautiful than the destination. Most of the people do not live in the present. They stay in the past or the future but not where they belong. And in the process, they spend most of their life and in the end regret not being able to live. These thoughts were striking him hard and while he was at it, he opened his eyes.

To his surprise, he was standing on the ground and not floating in the air anymore. Sam was still not able to believe what just happened. It all happened in quick succession and seemed like a dream. He looked up and almost lost his breath. He just fell from a cliff and was now standing unscathed.

"What just happened? What did I just experience? Who was that old man? Did I just survive falling from such a height?

Sam was bewildered and still in shock. He stood there for a while and kept looking up. His eyes were searching for the old man and his mind fixated on his image which was now cemented in his memory.

There was a narrow water stream flowing behind him. The rain had stopped. This area looked very different from what Sam had been seeing for the past 5-6 days. This was full of greenery and small boulders.

A lot had happened in the past week, beyond his comprehensive abilities. He sat on a small boulder beside the water stream and looked around.

There was a strange calm, inside & outside. Sam did not know where to go from that point. Following the downflow of the water stream was the only logical way. The evening had almost befallen. Sam had no option but to spend the night under the open sky.

# CHAPTER 23

## *The Purpose*

**11th June 2018**

Thankfully, the sky was clear tonight and stars were visible. Sam laid on the grass and looked up. Sam had a blissful, trance-like experience today when that old man had touched him.

He was still under the influence as if down a full bottle of whiskey. No drink, no activity ever brought him the joy which that experience brought to him.

He did not know what it was, but he was certain, he wanted it back and forever. And at that moment, his longing to be back to his old world and get reunited with his friends and family started to fade. He no longer wanted his old life back. His attachments & bondages with people and things did not seem strong enough to pull him back. It all felt so meaningless.

Sam's mind was now fixated to bring that inner peace and blissful experience and longing for it. He soon slept with that thought.

In his deep sleep, which he had after many days now, he found himself at the same place where he first encountered that old man in his dreams.

Sam was standing on a hillock, and a river was flowing down. There was a small cave behind him. Sun had started to set down. The meeting of the Sun with the horizon was creating a beautiful picture in the sky. Sun rays seemed like fire burning in the sky.

There were birds in the sky going back to their nests. A slow breeze, which calmed the mind. It was a very satisfying sight to behold and stay in it forever.

Sam looked at all of it. There were no thoughts in his mind. His mind was still as if all memories of the past were washed away and there he was standing, thoughtless, memoryless, a human being with no emotions, no memories, like a clean slate.

Suddenly, someone tapped his shoulder from behind. Sam turned around to find that same old man in front of him.

"So here you are. I knew I shall find you here. Afterall, this is your destiny, your final home", the old man said smiling.

Sam did not say anything. He kept looking at him. The old man held Sam's arm and took him inside the cave. He made him seated in a corner and sat himself on a small rock. They both were looking at him. Sam had tears in his eyes. He did not know what he was crying about but he was content with the fact, he was home finally. He was home after many thousands of births and millions of years.

The old man was looking at Sam and smiling.

"You know Samrat. This is the destiny of every living being on the earth. Everyone has to come back to me, but the illusion binds them.

But only a handful realise it until they take thousands of births and suffer endlessly. Your quest & thirst to know yourself ends here. Your sufferings end now. Your purpose now is to free those souls which are trapped in the body and take them to their destiny. You are all powerful. You are not Samrat anymore. You are the universe. You are the divine", saying this the old man hugged Sam.

The entire cave lit as if hundreds of oil lamps were lit. There was no Sam nor the old man. What was remaining of both was an earthen lamp, shining and lighting the entire cave like a guiding light for those who are lost.

***

# CHAPTER 24

## *Role Reversal*

**11th June 2018**

Sam suddenly woke up from a loud thud sound. He rubbed his eyes and looked around for the source of the sound. It was completely dark all around as it was still midnight. He saw a big tree floating in the river. It was uprooted and fell into the river from the hill.

But that was not the only reason for Sam to wake up. That dream woke him up. The tree falling into the river was a mere coincidence. It was very cold weather, but Sam was sweating. He was feeling intoxicated as if someone drugged him. He was not able to move, and he chose to lie down. The words of the old man were resonating in his mind.

"Who am I? Who is that old man? What is my connection with him? These questions were wobbling in his mind. The thought of going back or being rescued had vanished now. Sam did not know what to believe anymore.

The chirping sound of birds broke his sleep. They were sitting around him without any fear. Sam got up but they did not move. A sparrow flew and sat on his shoulder. Sam was surprised to see this and was wondering why they do not fear.

He got up and realised there was no pain in his hand and legs. He looked at his feet to check for wounds and bleeding but there was none. As if, he was never hurt. He was healed completely.

Sam walked up to the river. He sat down, took some water in his hand and washed his face. Sam was not able to recognize himself. His clothes were torn from many places.

He saw his reflection in the water. His beard had grown unusually big. It had become thick and long. He was amused to see a lot of grey hairs. He did not have a single grey hair until a week back. But his face had no sign of tiredness. His face was vibrating, and his eyes were fiery red. He could feel an exuberance of energy in his body.

This was very unusual. Sam's mind was still and there was no dilemma any further or any doubt. He thought about his life in Delhi, but it seemed as if his memories were being taken away from him. He could not remember much about it.

"Am I going crazy? Am I hallucinating? What is happening to me?", Sam told himself looking at his reflection in the river.

He was not able to recognize his own body and the new thoughts that were overpowering the older version of him.

‘Why don’t I want to go back? What happened to that new Car? What about the trip to Mauritius? Career, girlfriend, marriage, kids, why am I not able to think of any of these things? Why is my mind taking me back to this place? Why am I losing interest in everything that gave me so much pleasure and joy earlier?”, Sam was wondering while sitting beside the river.

He got up and started walking towards the forest. There was a small trail that he could find and follow. The forest was not as treacherous as it was up the hill. However, the narrow trail he followed was taking him inside the forest.

All the trees were looking fresh and soaked wet in the recent rain. Tree leaves were looking greener than ever and there was an enigmatic smell all around. A strange silence but Sam could hear a strange voice as if the forest would speak to him. He felt a strong connection with his surroundings and was observing, seeing, hearing & smelling things that he could never feel earlier.

This change was baffling for him. More than ‘How’, the ‘Why’ was a puzzle. But there was a newfound peace that surpassed all puzzling questions. He kept walking and, on his way, he found many wild animals but to his shock & surprise, none of them came near to him and those who did, behaved as if he is one of them.

As Sam walked further, that narrow stream of the river started to turn into a mighty river. He could see the smoke rising from a distance and some dwellings. It looked like a small village.

"Finally,", Sam said with a smile and took a deep breath. He looked up with teary eyes and folded hands. He started pacing towards the small huts in that village. As he reached the village, he found some men sitting around a bonfire. They looked at him and stood up. They folded their hands and bent forward as a sign of respect.

Sam thought it must be a local ritual to welcome a traveller or anyone new to the village.

"What is this place", Sam asked them.

"This is Pala village", a villeager replied.

"Which is the nearest town from here?", Sam asked.

"There is a small town, Kharsara. It's nearby. If you follow this trail and walk for an hour, you will reach there", that villager pointed in a direction.

"But, Yogiraj, where do you want to go?", another villager from the group asked Sam.

Yogiraj? This word hit Sam as hard as the rocks hit him while he was falling last night from the downhill.

"My name is Samrat", he said.

Everyone looked at each other and smiled looking at Sam. Sam could not understand this gesture. They again folded their hands and bent forward and went back to the bonfire.

Sam went in the direction, that villager had pointed earlier.

"Why did they address me as Yogiraj? He recalled his reflection from the river. Long, thick, grey beard, indeed made him look like a recluse and a lone wanderer. He shrugged off the thought and continued to walk on the trail, which was slowly becoming a muddy road, perhaps connecting the village to Kharsara town.

After walking for nearly one hour, Sam could indeed see some houses and a concrete road. He took the concrete road and went inside the town. It had started to drizzle so he took shelter inside a grocery store.

There was a small mirror in the general store. Sam chanced to look at himself in the mirror and then he got the reason for the tag Yogiraj, which he was given by those villagers. His hair was dishevelled, the beard had grown and turned grey.

"Who is this guy?", Sam murmured in shock.

"How far is Badrinath from here?", Sam asked the shopkeeper.

"It is very far from here, Baba", the shopkeeper replied.

Baba! This was another adjective Sam had received today. He ignored it and he knew the reason.

"How can I get there?", Sam asked.

"There is a bus which goes in the evening to Rudraprayag. The bus stop is just a few steps ahead. Once in Rudraprayag, you can take a taxi from there to Badrinath", the shopkeeper replied and got busy attending to a customer.

Sam looked at the watch on the wall in front of him. It was showing at 3 PM.

"What time does the bus leave?", Sam asked again.

'Usually, it comes around 4 PM. But you should go there and wait as sometimes, it comes early and leaves.

Sam was wondering why he asked about Badrinath and why not Delhi. He had a strong craving and urge to go to Badrinath and had lost all interest to be back to his old life in Delhi. He had lost sense of all possessions and was not interested in running for it anymore.

Drizzle had stopped and suddenly the weather had turned sunny. Sun had come out of the clouds. Sam started to walk towards the direction of the bus stand as suggested by the shopkeeper.

A few kids were playing nearby and they started to follow Sam. They were shouting something in their local language. Sam turned around and they all suddenly stopped where they were.

Baba, baba, baba, all the kids started to shout. Sam kept standing there and looked at them. They had encircled Sam and were shouting baba, baba, baba. Sam gave an angry look to those kids, and they dispersed shouting baba, baba.

Sam reached the bus stop and sat there. It was a small shed and was empty.

Sam sat there waiting for the bus. Earlier, whenever Sam got some time to sit and reflect, his mind started playing his memories like a flash and in fast forward and in an interwoven manner. But today, there were no memories, no past. He could sense his emotions, but they did not affect him like they used to.

He was observing his thoughts like a passing thought. He could hear the sound of bells from a nearby temple.

He started to wonder what people think when they visit a temple, a gurdwara, a mosque or a church. How can they find God in those places if they are never disconnected from the false reality? For them, the world is not an illusion but a wholesome place which they experience. So how would they experience a higher power if they don't realise the fickle nature of this reality and the nothingness of it.

"All my life, I have been oblivious to this, rather I lived in absolute oblivion. And now when I am starting to know the reality, it is all very overwhelming.

The enlightenment hits hard to whosoever achieves it. A whole life to unlearn and a whole life to learn nothing anymore. The realisation of knowing nothing and the reality of not knowing anything.

The honking of the bus woke him up from his thoughts.

He asked the bus conductor if the bus goes to the Rudraprayag to which the conductor nodded his head in agreement. Sam boarded the bus. It was almost empty barring 3 passengers occupying the front seats and one sitting at the rear end.

"Sir, ticket", Conductor gave Sam the ticket to Rudraprayag. Sam did not know how he would pay for the bus fare. He reached out to his trousers pocket to find something and there he found a Rs 100 note. Sam never kept money in his trousers pockets and always used a wallet. So, Sam had known now, this world is an illusion and he can create whatever he desires.

Sam went straight to the rear end of the bus. A man was looking outside the window. Sam looked at him and shouted in Joy mixed with Anger, "Anand!"

That guy looked at Sam and gave him a surprised look.

"Who are you and how do you know my name?", Anand asked.

"I am Sam. Remember me? You had left me there to die", Sam said with a mysterious smile on his face.

"Sam! Is it really you?", Anand got up and touched Sam's face and hugged him tight. Anand started to sob.

"I am sorry buddy. I am extremely sorry. I am so very happy to see you again. And you look so different, but I am glad you made it".

Sam looked at Anand and said, "No need to be sorry Anand. Had you not left me there, I would not have been here. I am not the same Sam you had met".

"What do you mean Sam?", Anand asked.

"After you left me in that snowstorm, I tried to find my way and got injured and later lost consciousness. A guy, named Bhaskar saved me and took me to a hut someplace far from there. And since then, a lot of things have happened.

I cannot blame you for anything. Everything was already planned it seems and it was my destiny. Meeting you then and now, it was all planned and destined", Sam said in a soft tone smiling.

Anand who was listening to all this was shocked. He was dumbfounded.

"Seems like, change of places", Anand said, winking at Sam.

They both started to laugh.

"But where are you going? What are you doing here?", Sam asked Anand.

"Sam, I have not been able to be at peace with myself after what happened that day. I cannot express my happiness seeing you alive and healthy. I went to the local rescue centre and informed them about the accident. Those guys tried for 4 days but in vain. Maybe they are still searching. I did not want to just sit and wait to hear bad news, so I started to look for you on my own", Anand replied.

"You were right about the nothingness of this life and the world, Anand", Sam said. "Will you believe, I met a yogi, supposedly the one who haunted me in real life and in my dreams before I decided to come here. My life changed after my encounter with him. I could now understand everything you told me. And I am very sorry for making fun of you. I was ignorant and naive."

"Everyone is naive until one day, the truth appears most bizarrely. Your encounter with the supreme was your destiny and here you are, full of wisdom, ready to spread the light, ready to become a beacon", Anand said looking at Sam.

"Am I really ready Anand? Don't I have to know anything further? What is next?", Sam sounded puzzled.

"The journey has just begun Sam. Don't worry nor think about the destination. It will appear on its own. Find yourself first. Be the Yogi", Anand replied.

'Be the Yogi'. These words hit Sam like a rock.

"Who is a Yogi Anand?", Sam asked Anand with a childlike curiosity.

Anand looked at Sam in his eyes and said, "**A yogi is the one who knows the futility of the world.** Who is always here but always one with the universe. A yogi is an observer and not the participant in this world. A yogi is not a character here but the director, who creates the movie people want to watch. A yogi knows why he or she is here.

*To be a yogi means to live without the coffins that people build around themselves. Yoga means union. It means you have breached the boundaries of the physical and have the ability to touch and experience everything in the universe. Unless a human being acquires this quality, they are somehow trying to hide from life", Anand replied.*

All your life, you were indulged in this world and were suffering in your own way. No experience lasted for more than a second or even less. You spent your whole life trying to recreate that experience but failed miserably and started to live in the past, trying to recreate a past.

So, nothing is permanent in this world. But there is something which is definitely permanent and that is a divine blessing, and I am sure you got a glimpse of it.

We are all past otherwise. But a yogi is not the past. He or she knows the past, present and future and goes beyond the boundaries of life, death and physical body. Be a yogi Sam, be the light for the people who are trapped, who have this veil over the mind, free them from the slavery of their mind and body".

Sam was listening to Anand with patience. He did not ask anything further nor replied. He just kept sitting and stared outside the window.

Sam did not know where he wanted to go now. Badrinath, Delhi, Rudraprayag or anywhere else.

The bus suddenly stopped. It was not any village or any town or any scheduled stop. The road ahead had caved in due to a landslide. Sam looked at Anand and they both smiled.

Sam got off the bus. He turned around, looked at Anand one last time and tore off the bus ticket and started to walk uphill.

Anand was looking at Sam, going away and kept looking at him until he faded away completely into nothingness.

# CHAPTER 25

## *Being Yogi...*

**18th October 2021**

The local newspaper of Rishikesh had the following news published on the 3rd page in a small corner.

"*A group of college students, stuck in a landslide, was saved by an old man who disappeared shortly after saving them.*

*There are many survivor stories about that old man who has saved several people. These survivors describe him as someone who has the body of a young boy but has a long grey beard and red fiery eyes. He appears from nowhere and disappears as fast as he had appeared. People have also claimed they saw him floating in the air and shining like a ball of fire.*

*However, people under trauma can experience hallucination so the truth in these stories cannot be confirmed*".

In the quest of *being yogi, the* seeker had realised his purpose. His journey was completed. He was finally home.